SPIRITUAL •
Companions

To Joan Spano —
With Affection
Padraic O'Hare

Jews, Christians, and Interreligious Relations

PADRAIC O'HARE

TWENTY
THIRD *23rd*
PUBLICATIONS

Twenty-Third Publications
A Division of Bayard
One Montauk Avenue, Suite 200
New London, CT 06320
(860) 437-3012 or (800) 321-0411
www.twentythirdpublications.com
ISBN-10: 1-58595-522-1
ISBN: 978-1-58595-522-0

Library of Congress Catalog Card Number: 2005929734
Printed in the U.S.A.

Dedication

Foreword

Padraic O'Hare is a veteran of the Jewish-Christian dialogue. For many years, he has faithfully represented his own Roman Catholic tradition in the precious encounter with Jewish figures—an encounter which has done so much to heal the historic breach of Christian anti-Judaism. When the dialogue began more than a generation ago, in the searing aftermath of the Holocaust, the idea was that two alienated peoples would overcome hostility with understanding, even love. The main effect of dialogue, it was assumed, would be each party's achievement of new appreciation and respect for the other's basic beliefs. But the effect of dialogue, as it turned out, was more far-reaching than that. In the presence of the other—so it seems to this Christian—each partner found it necessary to examine those very beliefs, precisely in the light of how they affected the other.

Dialogue entered a new stage. Moving from civil exchanges between two separate groups, focused on a sharing of dogmas and traditions that were assumed to be beyond criticism, dialogue became the self-critical examination of one's own dogma and tradition in the presence of the other, and in the light of the other's experience and belief. In this book, Padraic O'Hare gives us an exemplary version of that process. *Spiritual Companions* is an act of Catholic theological self-criticism undertaken in the spiritual presence of the covenant God makes with Israel—in the presence, that is, of the religious commitment to which Jesus of Nazareth remained faithful until the day he died; and in the presence of the living witness of the rabbinic Judaism that has flourished down through the centuries. Thus, for example, O'Hare not only retrieves the Christian genius of St. Augustine and Thomas Merton, say, but measures it against the genius of Rabbis Abraham Joshua Heschel and Joseph Soloveitchick.

In dialogue with the other—again, speaking from the Christian side—one comes face to face with one's own responsibility for the accidents and offenses of history. But repentance is not enough. O'Hare shows how a full and honest encounter with the deeply held beliefs and experiences of another tradition requires a re-examination of one's own deeply held beliefs. In the case of Judaism, Christians have already begun to move away from the "replacement" theology according to which the "new Israel" (the Church) has superseded the "old Israel." Certainly Roman Catholicism, with the milestone declarations of the Second Vatican Council, has honored Judaism precisely by revising the basic theological claims that were the source of anti-Jewish denigration. Vatican II was the beginning of a process, not the end. What O'Hare shows in this book is what such a work of theological re-envisioning looks like when it is carried forward with unflinching honesty, respectful of the tradition but also open to what in the tradition must be changed. O'Hare is a faithful son of Vatican II.

This is an informed and lucid book. The necessary history is here. So is a full appreciation of the glories of the Christian past. But what makes this work illuminating is the fact that it is written from within a profound religious commitment. O'Hare remembers what religion is for: not to honor dogma or belief; not to worship the altar. Religion is for honoring God. Religion worships not itself, but God. Religion worships, that is, not the altar, but at the altar. It seems obvious to say so, but—such is the human condition of the religious condition—religion keeps forgetting that.

When religious people make absolutes of the signs and sacraments that intend to point beyond themselves to the One who alone is absolute, tragic—often violent—consequences follow. History is full of those stories—and so, for that matter, are today's newspapers. But the very shape of this book represents the answer to that problem, for O'Hare moves from an examination of tradition and a re-envisioning of theology, both in the light of insights born of dialogue, to a firm proclamation of the centrality of prayer. Praying together can be a fulfillment of dialogue. The very structure of this book shows that faith is rational, and that critical thought, embodied in theological exchange, is essential to it. But the book shows that thought opens into something else: the sacred world of contemplation.

In contemplation, O'Hare teaches, one encounters God in all mystery. God is the radically Other, the One who can never be known except in the act of unknowing. Knowledge is preparation for the holy unknowing that is the opposite of ignorance. Therefore every religious affirmation, every dogma, and every aspect of the revered tradition is in itself incomplete. That very incompleteness is the revelation. Here, above all, is what Christians have learned from Jews. Only God is complete, which is another way of saying, only God is God. Shema, Israel! Jesus comes to point not to himself, but to the One whom he calls Father. In that we see the full Jewishness of Jesus.

A feeling for this mystery is itself the correction of religious triumphalism. What Padraic O'Hare shows with rare eloquence and reverence is that the new way into this holy of holies is through the precious encounter of believers who approach the mystery differently, but recognize together the one God.

— James Carroll
Author, *Constantine's Sword: The Church and the Jews*

Précis

This book is animated by the belief that people in any religious community, on any spiritual path, can be enriched by clues to living spiritual lives from people in religious communities and spiritual ways other than their own, and that this need not undermine people's rootedness. Its thesis is that people in every religious community, on every spiritual path, should come to practice spiritual companionship, to encounter one another as siblings—all God's children—and our ways of faithfulness should, as far as possible, become transparent to one another.

In articulating this thesis, the book employs the relations between Jews and Christians as, in some measure, a model and example, and treats the current status of these relations. It deals with the problems attending this thesis, the theology of revelation underpinning it, an appreciation of Christianity as an example of it, and a model of contemplation education as the practice for achieving it. It shows how to approach teaching and learning about one another in ways that foster reverence.

Contents

Foreword by James Carroll   v

Précis   ix

Chapter One: Companions Searching in the Wilderness   1

Chapter Two: What Is Achieved, What Remains   30

Chapter Three: Revelation Is No Thing   75

Chapter Four: How Reverence Emerges   99

Chapter Five: Praying Together   126

Epilogue: Education for Reverence   140

Acknowledgments   145

Index   148

Companions Searching in the Wilderness

Personal Journey

The thesis of this book is, to me, so problematic, and at the same time so compelling, that I think it is necessary to begin by framing the passion which gives rise to the book with personal experience. This is not an approach I would ordinarily take. Everything that I've written about has engaged me passionately and in this sense may be personal. But here, for the first time in my professional life (including publishing essays, reviews, books, and collections over twenty-five years), I think that speaking directly of personal experience will help the reader understand. Whether it persuades is another matter.

The "wilderness" in the title of this chapter is my wilderness; the "searching" my searching. I don't mean anything melodramatic by calling my life a wilderness. Neither does the metaphor point to a life more tragic than others. Every woman and man's life is a wilderness, if by wilderness we understand that everyone is subject to suffering, every life is to some extent restless, every life is hidden in part to itself, all human relations are subject to "cobweb[s] on the soul."[1]

There is a "dying" to small self which many spiritual geniuses recommend; dying to the self which suffers, the self which is restless and subject to alienation and illusion. The dying is surely the gateway to happiness. It leads to "purity of heart," sometimes, but not exhaustively, associated with "apatheia": "a relatively permanent state of deep calm resulting from the integration of the emotional life under the influence of agape."[2]

But this dying is not easy work. Jesus of Nazareth said we have to die if we are to be reborn, and Saint Paul that we must be crucified with Christ so it is Christ who lives in us.[3] The Zen master, Shunryu Suzuki says: "In order to live in the realm of Buddha nature, it is necessary to die as a small being moment by moment."[4] Sufi literature records the wisdom that we should die before we die. And Bede Griffiths, invoking the wisdom of Hinduism and speaking of the difficulty of uniting the small self (*jivatman*) with the Great Self (*Atman*) as a figurative "fall," (life in the wilderness banished from Eden) says "The fall is the fall into self consciousness, that is into a consciousness centered in the self which has lost touch with the eternal ground of consciousness, which is the true Self."[6]

Compassion is one of the great products of this dying, coming in from the wilderness of self-centeredness. And yet, Thomas Merton calls compassion "my new desert," a dry and punishing place.[7] This coming in from the wilderness is not easy.

Searching is tantamount to living well, to living a reflective life, to living a spiritual life. Merton writes that spiritual life is first of all a life.[8] What "searching" or "spiritual" add to "life" is the connotation that one is paying attention to their lives, to what they are becoming, to the kinds of lives they are sculpting. (Later in this chapter I will fill this in a bit more and employ the idea of "faithfulness" to the human vocation.)

By calling my life a searching life, I mean nothing terribly narcissistic. In fact, to say so, to call my life a searching life, floods me with gratitude and with humility. Humility, a sense of truthfulness, that my searching life, the opposite of a life of drift, is so little a product of my own authorship and so much the product of influences for which I am not worthy and therefore especially grateful. These influences include a certain kind of a parent, a certain kind of a teacher, a certain kind of spouse, a certain kind of son, a certain kind of friend.

The personal experience I want to share which animates this book is the profound influence during the last twenty years of Judaism and of Buddhism on my search in the wilderness, and how these influences have fully enriched my Catholicism. Mine is an experience like Raimundo Panikkar's of which he writes: "I left [Europe] as a Christian, I 'found' myself a Hindu, and I 'returned' a Buddhist without having ceased to be a Christian."[9]

The experience leads me to believe that people in any religious community and spiritual path can be enriched by clues to living spiritual lives from both practices and beliefs native to religious communities and spiritual ways other than their own. And further, this need not undermine people's rootedness in their religious communities of primary affiliation. Finally, people in every religious community deserve to be exposed to clues perhaps more richly etched and practiced in other spiritual ways. And each and every religious community should sponsor interreligious encounter of this kind in this sense.

During the last twenty years, my escalating exposure to Jews and Judaism has taught me a rich new way to be a Christian, specifically a Catholic. A spotty but deepening study of biblical, historical, and contemporary religious, moral, and cultural Judaism has grown together with a more substantial study of the history and theological justifications of Christian antisemitism and what they demand of Christian religious educators and theologians. Alongside these developments, inextricable but more important than either of them, I have during these years befriended and been befriended by a small legion of Jewish women and men who continue to teach me lessons in humor, intellectual integrity, moral sensitivity, and humanity.

By humanity I mean kindness. Philo of Alexandria, known as well to history as Philo the Jew, wrote the immortal words, "Be kind, for everyone you meet is fighting a great battle."[10] Moral sensitivity evokes a Jewish acquaintance who, after his deceased and revered father ranks

Isaiah the Prophet and Pope John XXIII his second and third heroes of repair of the world (*tikkun olam*). This man embodies their ideals in his human practice in business, politics, philanthropy, and personal life.

Conrad Hyers speaks of humor "in the midst of conflict and anxiety, success and failure, faith and doubt...com[ing] to terms...with the ambiguities and ambivalence of the human situation...with absurdity, evil, suffering and death."[11]

Clearly my further instruction in humor (for it is, also, my childhood birthright), has not been a minor theme. For this and many blessings, I give thanks for the late Rabbi Murray Rothman, one of whose invaluable contributions to my life has been to share with me this truth: that life is a river, or maybe it's not a river.

I said that Jews and Judaism have taught me a rich, renewed way to be a Christian, to be a Catholic. Building on a foundation of conciliar Catholic theology (the theology of the Second Vatican Council, which is itself indebted to Jewish influence), Jewish life and thought have enhanced my sense of the Church as a community and of moral life as balancing individual and common goods. Even shifts in my view of Jesus Christ, beyond the study of the "Jewishness of Jesus," and touching the central idea and experience of incarnation itself, show a Jewish influence. I have in mind here not only the doctrine of the Incarnation, least of all in its docetic expression (where the emphasis on Jesus' divinity virtually denies his humanity). Rather, my continued embrace of (and by) Jews and Judaism reveals to me ever deepening layers of the incarnational spirit or ethos: that the divine and the human are locked in intimate embrace and human transcending, moving toward the Holy One. (I will say more about these theological influences in chapter four).

So it is that several years before I read David Tracy's characterization of liberation theology (with its view of communal Church, social morality, and truly human Christ), as a re-Judaizing of Christianity,[12] I was already well on my way to understanding Jews and Judaism as defining influences for Christianity to be faithful to the God of Israel.[13]

During roughly the same twenty-year period, my life has been deeply enriched by increasing study and appreciation of Buddha and Buddhism, especially Zen practice. This has assisted me profoundly to pray the

Christian prayer of silence employing technique derived from practice of *zazen* (Zen seated meditation). This is so important to my well-being and what social harmony I promote that it truly validates Rabbi Heschel's remark that prayer "saves the inner life from oblivion."[14]

Of course I am not alone in having been attracted to Buddhist practice in the last twenty years. The movement of Westerners to incorporate this practice into their lives in other religious communities, or, more controversially, to replace earlier religious affiliation, is the subject of much commentary, some of it negative, even ridiculing. This is all fine where "good trees" do not bear "good fruit," where so-called Buddhist practice finds exhaustive expression in greater personal equanimity but no greater justice, forgiveness, or compassion.

But the easy dismissal of Buddhist meditative practice as a fad is really deeply ignorant and represents a somewhat jaded failure to notice the profundity of the simple, in this instance, the elemental simplicity of seated practice. For in a world filled with people who think they know a great deal (much of which turns out to be illusory), Buddhist practice invites us to stop, to sit well and comfortably, to breathe deeply, calmly, peacefully so we can return to the present moment in silence. In this way we purify consciousness and perception, we are enabled to act compassionately, and we more fully celebrate life's joys and bear with its sorrows.[15]

This is prayer focused especially on inner life and on stillness. There is also the Western Christian apophatic (negative, silent, imageless) tradition of contemplative practice from which the prayer of silence comes. This provides a route from within Christianity to some of the same fruits as Zen practice offers. Still, anyone who has stayed with the simple disciplines of such practice—the posture, the breathing, the patient, sustained sitting long enough to experience deepening levels of presence, silence, and peace, and rising from sitting to act more gently and kindly—such a one will know how precious Zen and other forms of Buddhist practice can be to anyone, regardless of the religious community in which they are especially rooted.

The immanence of the divine, a defining idea of the Catholic incarnational spirit, is what is in play when we give priority to the importance of meditative prayer. The process itself is nothing less than revelatory. In Roger Haight's words (on revelation) we are "welcoming in receptivity the self-communication of the divine."[16] And Augustine, writing in a distinctively "Catholic" tone, recommends the importance of meditative prayer when he writes "Descend into thy self, go into the inner recesses of thy mind. If thou be far from thy self how can thou be near to God?"[17]

It remains to say that each element of this experience, my own enrichment by Judaism and by Buddhism, as well as the capacity to integrate these influences in an enriched Catholicism, is associated in a special way with a great spiritual teacher from each tradition.

It will become clear shortly, and throughout this book, how great an influence Rabbi Abraham Joshua Heschel has in my life. With regard to Buddhism, Thay (teacher) Thich Nhat Hanh occupies a similar place. This book does not deal with Buddhist-Christian relations. In two earlier works of mine, however, which lay out a program and theological foundation for giving priority to contemplation education in the lives of people in religious communities, his influence is clearly evident.[18]

It is above all to Father "Louie," to Thomas Merton, that I turn each day for wisdom to live a spiritual life in a Christian key. Later in this book, I will explore Merton's place as a uniquely honest, expert, and fearless exemplar for persons in many religious communities, on many spiritual paths. Merton, it seems to me, is "right" about so many things needed to live lives that are faithful to the human vocation. Not the least of his gifts was to see so clearly and express so articulately the richness available through interreligious encounter.

Thesis

I've already said that this book is animated by the belief "that people in any religious community or any spiritual path can be enriched by clues to living spiritual lives...from religious communities and spiritual ways other than their own...[that] this need not undermine people's rootedness....that people deserve to be exposed to [other] clues [and that]...each religious community should sponsor interreligious encounters of this kind...."

Framed even more directly, the thesis of this work is that people in every religious community, on every spiritual path, should come to practice spiritual companionship, to encounter one another as siblings—all God's children—and our ways of faithfulness should, as far as possible, become transparent to one another. In a word, we should pray together as well as separately. In Rabbi Heschel's words, we need one another "to search in the wilderness for wellsprings of devotion, for treasures of stillness, for the power of love and care for man...to cooperate in trying to bring about a resurrection of sensitivity, a revival of conscience."[19]

The problems attending this thesis will be touched on below and dealt with at length in chapters two, three, and four. These problems, as I said in the first sentence of this book, are profound. And yet surely there is a simple truth in Leonard Swidler's observation that "Everyone searching for religious meaning and truth, no matter how convinced by and committed to a particular tradition or position, if they would act with integrity must have a radical openness."[20]

The thesis calls us beyond what so many of its finest participants seem to envision by "dialogue."[21] This is certainly true of much theological dialogue between Jews and Christians, perhaps less so in conversations between Buddhists and some Christians.

The need to go beyond dialogue of a certain kind can be seen in the framing of boundaries of dialogue by so advanced a practitioner as David Novak, of whose work more will be said in chapter two. For now I note his initial remarks in an excellent volume of reflections by Jewish scholars and rabbis called *Christianity in Jewish Terms*. Despite the sensitivity of so many of the contributions, as well as the basic intent of the book, the text nevertheless begins with Novak's caution that there can be no fudging of truth claims in interreligious dialogue, for after all, "Some things are true all the time, everywhere and for everyone."[22]

How different this is from Rabbi Heschel's words "that the most significant basis for the meeting of men of different religious traditions is the level of fear and trembling...humility and contrition...where all formulations...appear as understatements...," and our souls "stripped of pretensions and conceit...we sense the tragic insufficiency of human faith."[23]

Theological dialogue seems so often to end at the water's edge of protecting truth claims. It would be a great mistake, however, to alienate the processes of searching the wilderness together (a process that takes us beyond guarding truth claims to common prayer), from engagement together in theological discourse or dialogue. The desert father Evargrius Ponticus said, "If you are a theologian you truly pray, [and] if you truly pray you are a theologian."[24] And I am certain Rabbi Heschel had something similar in mind in distinguishing "theology" from "depth theology."[25]

The possible complimentarity of theological dialogue and a fuller spiritual companionship is no where to date, to my knowledge, better displayed than in the encounters achieved in the Catholic-Jewish Colloquium conceived and conducted over two years (1993-95) by Mary C. Boys and Sara Lee. These meetings engaged twenty-two Jewish and Catholic educators in six two-day-long sessions. Boys writes of them: "For Colloquium participants the ties of friendship meant a serious investment in the health of the other's faith traditions...," and that participants in the Colloquium experienced "the virtues of friendship—patience, hard work, humility [and] 'holy envy' (experiencing something so profound in the beliefs, rituals or practices of another tradition that one wishes his or her own community of faith also had or practiced it....)"[26]

(The "holy envy" referred to is pivotal to achieving spiritual companionship. The term was coined by the great ecumenist and Scripture scholar, Krister Stendahl, who sees its presence "when we recognize something in another tradition that is beautiful but is not ours, nor should we grab it or claim it....Holy envy rejoices in the beauty of the other.")[27]

Nowhere in the report of Colloquium sessions is the efficacy of these encounters more evident, their likely evolution over the course of the meetings from theology to depth theology, from "mere dialogue" to something deeper, than in these words of David Ellenson, a Jewish theologian associated with the project: "The Colloquium was a profoundly religious experience; it drew its participants into the boundlessness of the Divine. It challenged participants to move beyond the narrow limits in which they confine the Holy One to acknowledge in their heart of hearts that God, the Mother and Father of all of us, has many children...."[28]

Ellenson's words are remarkably consonant with David Tracy's assertion that "the praxis of interreligious dialogue itself, I believe does not merely bear a 'religious dimension.' It is a religious experience."[29] And Boys writes of her own hopes and expectations for dialogue that is "an encounter with the religious 'other,' the 'stranger' [and] is a catalyst for continuing religious conversion because it throws one upon the graciousness of God, the Wholly Other in our midst."[30]

I mention the possible complimentarity of theological dialogue and spiritual companionship which seems to be expressed in the Colloquium meetings. My caution is based on two factors. First, to my knowledge, very few if any interreligious theological dialogues are informed by the educational sophistication which Boys and Lee brought to these meetings. I share a pedigree with Mary Boys; we both studied religious education with many of the same masters. Boys cites one of them, Dwayne Hubner, reflecting the educational practice with which she and Lee sough to underpin the theological dialogue which they sponsored (the quotes within quotes are Hubner's words): "We might think of education as the 'meeting of the historically determined self with the new, the strange, the strangers' in such a way that the profound longing and thirst central to human life are 'recognized as the source and goal of life.'"[31]

These words point to a very profound practice of education, one in which education means relationships between people (and also beyond human exchanges alone), relationships that are intrinsically religious. In this view, nothing less than our faithfulness to the human vocation is at issue in educational practice. Such practice is transformative; there is always some conversion going on. But theological dialogues which are not framed and informed by such profound education practice run the risk of stopping at the edge. However deep the learning and sincere the will to speak and listen well, these dialogues may end, in the phrase of Juan Luis Segundo, in the exchange of "mere erudition." They may remain, as Cardinal Newman said, "notional" rather than "real."

The second caution arises from a feature of Mary Boys' own reflection on the Catholic-Jewish Colloquium and its larger educational context. This occurs in a chapter of her remarkable work, *Has God Only One Blessing? Judaism As a Source of Christian Self Understanding.* The chapter is a thoughtful reflection on re-education, on conversion or transformation, resulting from dialogue. It relies in part and significantly on the ideas of Bernard Lonergan and those of Walter Conn, and reports substantially, though in part, on the series of meetings between 1993 and 1995. It is, however, principally about the conversion of attitudes of the Christian participants in the Colloquium, though clearly Jewish participants were deeply moved as David Ellenson's words make clear, and which will be attested again when I return to a discussion of the Colloquium in the Epilogue of this work. This is not cited as fault. Like my own 1997 book on Jewish-Christian relations, Boys' text, published in 2000 CE, is chiefly directed at repairing Christian attitudes. However, the tenor of the chapter, suggestively called "Re-Educating Ecclesia," pinpoints at least one ambiguity about the relationship between theological dialogue and achieving spiritual companionship.

Problems

I am tempted (in fact, I have succumbed to the temptation), to begin this section by citing Rabbi Heschel's uproarious observation about a man with no problems. Heschel says that "man has problems. Even God has problems. [But]…here stands a man…who has no problems! Do you know why? He's an idiot!"[32]

As noted, this is only the first, brief, rendition of the range of problems of which the author is aware that attend the thesis of this book. It seems to me I must attach a magical power to intoning these caveats as if the more I do so the more I change the odds affirming the possibility of evolution to a stage of spiritual companionship among people in various religious communities, on different spiritual paths. Here I treat in brief five problems associated with the general thesis of this book, problems in sharing clues to spiritual living across any potential pairing of religious communities and spiritual ways and five problems specific to deepening the encounter between Jews and Christians.

The first general problem is that there is no paradigm modeling the way in which significant numbers in any two religious communities might achieve deep levels of encounter with one another beyond dialogue. There are examples of deep interreligious encounter that may or may not serve as paradigms or models for broader movements, and there are many individual exemplars. Bede Griffiths comes to mind as an exemplar in Hindu-Christian relations. And Merton's appreciation of Zen and the influence of this appreciation in his writings on identity, self-consciousness, presence, and silence, are another example. There are also, as already noted in the discussion of the Catholic-Jewish Colloquium, some instances of a tantalizing "possible complimentarity," with spiritual companionship perhaps evolving from theological dialogue.

Finally, we have many heartening examples of members of different religious communities acting in common to serve persons through works of justice and of peace. I have argued elsewhere,[33] and still maintain, that this should not be held up as the end of interreligious encounter but a profound outcome of it. I will take up the issue again in chapter two.

Forging deep interreligious encounter is presumably linked to what participants perceive as the benefits. There seem to be two general possibilities here. Either we experience encounter as confirming and enriching elements that are prominent within our own religious community and its spiritual way, or we experience the enrichment of our religious community by the introduction of elements, of spiritual practice for example, that are not so well developed in our religious community. Paul Knitter's discussion of what he takes to be the uniqueness of John Cobb's approach to articulating theological grounds for embracing religious pluralism is instructive here. Knitter believes that unlike other prominent figures in this area of theological work, Cobb avoids the idea that "all religions have the same basic (or essential) task which each carries out with rough parity."[34] What is more attractive to Knitter in Cobb's approach is that it is based on the idea that "...all religions have different tasks."[35]

Whatever one makes of the distinction (to which we will return at the end of this chapter), neither approach assures achieving deep encounter or provides a paradigm overcoming the asymmetries between the parties to any possible pairing of significant numbers in any two religious communities.

The second general problem is that the thesis of this book is, on the face of it, utterly prescriptive. That is to say it isn't at all clear at the outset that what is advocated here, even if viewed positively, is actually attainable. In chapter two I cite the work of Fayette Breaux Veverke. She asks, suggestively, whether anyone or many people believe or can come to believe that building "bridges" is consistent with maintaining "boundaries." The problem is seen more sharply when we remember that the bridge whose construction, or expansion, is proposed here is the bridge to becoming spiritually transparent, as far as possible, to one another. This bridge is of far greater expanse than that of theological dialogue alone.

A third problem is that the call to find ways, as companions, to search in the wilderness together flies in the face of rising tides of religious fundamentalism in our day. Martin Marty and R. Scott Appleby's book, *Accounting for Fundamentalism*, helps dramatize the antithesis between the thesis of this book and the spirit of fundamentalism: "Fundamentalism appears as a strategy, or set of strategies, by which beleaguered believers attempt to preserve their distinctive identity as a people or a group...[from] outsiders who threaten to draw believers into a syncretistic...milieu."[36] In this milieu, advocates of dialogue are deeply suspect. How much more suspect are "co-religionists who appear to have adapted all too well to modernity through unholy compromise"[37] when the call is to spiritual encounter deeper than theological dialogue?

The companion problem to the rise in fundamentalism (and our fourth general problem) is the eclipse of the liberal theological imagination. This book is entirely a work of the liberal theological impulse, as is all interreligious engagement, provided the motives are sincere. In chapter two I will lay out in summary form, and in chapter four at length, the content of a liberal theological view of the defining symbols, practices and beliefs of Christians. Chapter three deals with the liberal theological view of the pivotal issue in all interreligious engagement at any level, the issue of revelation. The primary purpose of this exercise is to show the reader who is not Christian the richness of Christian belief when it is liberated from dogmatic obscurantism, cynical manipulation and intellectual naivete.

David Tracy provides a precise and persuasive definition of the liberal model of theological reflection. We are thinking in the liberal theological key when our work making religious experience intelligible is deeply influenced by historical consciousness and by the effort to discover contemporary patterns of common human experience. Historical consciousness might unearth the context out of which Catholics, for example, came to believe and teach that an all-loving God consigns unbaptized babies to Limbo for all eternity. Plumbing patterns of common human experience might cause the same (theologically liberal) person to abandon the teaching! Or, historical consciousness might unearth the origins and influences of patriarchy overshadowing the relative inclusiveness of the primitive Christian Jewish community. Attending to patterns of common human experience might cause people to reject the idea that God prefers men to women! This is the liberal impulse in religion and in theology; contrast it with Pope John Paul II speaking of "the noisy propaganda of liberalism, of freedom without truth or responsibility" and the problem crystallizes.[38]

A final general problem with the thesis of this book is that there continues to be so much interreligious strife, including violence, but also ignorant, negative stereotyping coming from sources least expected because presumed to be more sophisticated. An example of this back peddling can be found in recent Vatican characterizations of Buddhism.

In the last few years, Vatican officials have stumbled badly in caricaturing Buddhism. Though Pope John Paul II had a number of admiring things to say of Buddhism, his principal message with regard to this spiritual path was really a calumny, presumably unintended but hard to reconcile with the Pope's broad erudition. In his 1994 book, *Crossing the Threshold of Hope*,[39] the pope paints an erroneous and reductionistic picture of essential Buddhism as entirely inward and socially irresponsible. But the pope is topped by his intimate collaborator in triumphalism, Cardinal Joseph Ratzinger, now Pope Benedict XVI. In 1998 remarks, Ratzinger dismisses Buddhism as an "autoerotic spirituality."[40] Responding, Buddhist scholar and Buddhist Francis Cook notes the "linking [of] Buddhism with Onan's solitary vice and hinting in the strongest terms that both are wasting their time, to say the least."[41] Cook comments: "This is strange in the light of the atmosphere of the Second Vatican Council and its stated hopes for more respect and understanding, as well as for more dialogue. Which Vatican are we to believe?"[42]

What the pope and the cardinal are culpably ignorant of, or know but refuse to acknowledge, is the long and rich tradition, in Mahayana Buddhism especially, placing compassion (*karuna*) at the heart of Buddhist practice and setting the image of the Bodhisattva, the compassionate Buddha, on high for emulation. Cook is especially justified in asking which Vatican to believe. He has in mind a point of conciliar theology that the pope and cardinal dishonor. For it is in the Second Vatican Council's document, *Ad Gentes*, that we read that Christians "should carefully consider how traditions of asceticism and contemplation whose seeds have been sown by God in certain ancient cultures before the preaching of the Gospels might be incorporated into Christian religious life."[43]

Turning to the specific problems of Jewish-Christian relations, we need to begin by acknowledging the extraordinary repair of these relations since the middle of the last century. Reports of the eclipse of antisemitism will always be premature, but it is not useful to ignore the remarkable strides Jews and Christians have made together since the end of the Second World War. (That he fails to take account of this progress is one of the chief criticisms of Daniel Goldhagen and his book, *Moral Reckoning*).

I will detail the story of this progress in chapter two. But positive developments not withstanding, there is still a broad range of problems in these relations, problems which take on a special character when we look to deepen the encounter between Jews and Christians.

The first problem is our common history. In the late 1940s, the French Jewish philosopher Jules Issac gave this history the name "teaching of contempt." In his 1947 essay, "Has Anti-Semitism Roots in Christianity?" Issac identified eighteen elements in the centuries of Christian derogation of Jews, elements ranging from negative interpretations of the teachings of Hebrew scripture, through the decide charge (that the Jews murdered God), to the "de-Judaizing" of Jesus and more.[44] These and other teachings throughout the centuries gave rise to persecution and pogrom, inquisition and expulsion, forced conversion and auto da fe (public spectacles in which the sincerity of Jewish converts would be subjected to impossible tests; when the tests were failed, the Jews were executed). Thanks to the work of Robert Kertzer,[45] we now know that official Catholicism hammered this contemptuous teaching home until the very brink of the Holocaust, a horror that could not have occurred apart from the centuries of teaching contempt.

The reconciliation between so many Jews and Christians, our range of theological dialogues, and work in common to assist people to have justice and peace are themselves startling in the light of our shared history. One wonders what strains might be placed on relations by the effort to deepen these relations as profoundly as envisioned here by the effort to systematize a far broader and deeper spiritual encounter with one another.

The second and third problems are the facts of Jewish minority status and of Jewish assimilation.

A variety of historical, cultural, and ideological factors have combined to make Jews, in significant percentages, disproportionately effective and influential in a range of cultural, educational, and professional works. Among the historical factors is the very isolation to which Jews have been subjected from time to time throughout the centuries. Among the cultural and ideological factors is the power and importance traditional Jewish spiritual and moral teaching attaches to the mitzvoth of study. But, although prominent, Jewish women and men are very small minorities within populations in which they are numbered, save Israel. When we add to this the fact of precipitous assimilation rates of Jewish persons in countries like the United States, the grounds for resisting the practices advocated in this book become evident.

I think these factors are in play even where relations are at their best. Consider the scores of Jewish theological, educational, and rabbinic leaders who signed *Dabru Emet* ("A Jewish Statement on Christians and Christianity"). One of the "eight statements about how Jews and Christians may relate to one another" is this: "A new relationship between Jews and Christians will not weaken Jewish practices....An improved relationship will not accelerate the cultural and religious assimilation that Jews rightly fear. It will not change traditional forms of worship nor increase intermarriage between Jews and non-Jews, nor persuade more Jews to convert to Christianity, nor create a false blending of Judaism and Christianity."[46]

A powerful endorsement, at once cautious but unafraid. Yet, to me, the statement seems to presuppose that relations continue to consist chiefly of common ethical practice and sensitive theological discourse. I am not confident the statement would be made in front of a broad movement among Jews and Christians to do those things necessary to "search the wilderness" together, to share "wellsprings of devotion..." and "treasures of stillness," to do together things that require even more spiritual companionship and transparency.

The fourth special problem in deepening Jewish-Christian relations is of an entirely different kind from the first three. In an earlier formulation of the thesis of this book I said that people in one religious community can be enriched by "clues" in other religious communities. Under clues I included both "practices and beliefs." The fourth special problem has to do with the usefulness of Christian beliefs to Jewish companions in the proposed deeper encounter.

The issue is not whether it would enrich the life of a Jewish person to *believe* a Christian belief. With Michael Kogan, to whom we will have further reference in chapter two, I affirm that the adoption by Jews "...of any part of the kerygma [proclaimed message] of Christianity," is "inauthentic and unnecessary."[47] And Pope John Paul II affirms this same sentiment in effect when, over and over again, he refers to the Jewish people as "the people of the Old [sic] Covenant never revoked by God."[48] So it isn't a question of Jews believing what Christian believe, (or for that matter Muslims believing what Buddhists believe). The question is the possible *usefulness* of Christian beliefs for Jews (or

Buddhist beliefs for Muslims) and the problems that attach to this issue.

As noted earlier, the liberal theological perspective informs this book from beginning to end. In this view, the language of belief is analogical and metaphorical, not literal; its truth is existential and moral, not metaphysical. What is at issue when one asserts that the beliefs of members of one religious community might be useful to members of other religious communities is, first of all, whether others can understand the meaning of these beliefs as expressions of religious experience. If they can, then they may recognize comparable religious experiences, "theology" may become "depth theology," and they may be consoled by this experience of solidarity and common purpose with other spiritual seekers.

I hope the reader appreciates by now that for me clarifying the meaning of religious beliefs is not the chief instrument for deepening encounter. It is a work of theological dialogue that either short-circuits, ending with swapping "mere erudition," or leads beyond itself, transformed by common prayer, to spiritual companionship. Nevertheless, finding the body of convictions—the creedal element, the beliefs—of the others to some significant extent feasible, finding that these convictions point to and illumine some common religious experiences, seems at least very helpful.

But when we turn to this dimension, we are confronted with a great, thick edifice of Christian dogmatic positivism, obscurantism, and naïve realism. Many Christians, especially in the so-called "grand churches" like Catholicism with our elaborate doctrinal systems, have been so intent on defending antique and arcane language and interpretation of doctrines from ideological trends of the modern world and from one another, that we have rendered the meanings of these great Christian convictions virtually impenetrable to ourselves and certainly to people in other religious communities. Commenting on the causes for this, within historical Catholicism, Edward Schillebeeckx ascribes the syndrome to 500 years in thrall to "Cartesian dualism and post-Reformation defensiveness."[49]

I fully appreciated the thickness of this blockage when a Jewish friend and colleague, a man of learning and sensitivity, a theologian, a rabbinic leader and ecumenist, announced good-naturedly to a class-room of Christians I had asked him to address that there could be no incarnation in Judaism precisely because for Judaism everyone is an incarnation of the Divine. My friend was alluding, of course, to the doctrine of the incarnation, especially in its docetic form, in which the claim "Jesus Christ is God" is made without qualification or nuance. The meaning that was blocked, not only from my Jewish friend but also from many Christians, is the broadly incarnational spirit that is characteristic of a great deal of Christianity at its best, a meaning that is also present in christology proper. Of this dimension, John Macquarrie writes: "if we hold fast to the existential dimension in understanding christhood...we see christology as a kind of transcendental anthropology...[a view of human beings as *all* moving toward the Divine, which moves toward them]...with christhood as the goal toward which created existence moves."[50]

Karl Rahner has also, and famously, criticized how trinitarian language has evolved in Catholic doctrinal practice.[51] And I myself have heard spiritually and theologically sophisticated Christians employ the language "Father, Son and Holy Spirit" as if the language stipulates precisely who—the mysterious—God is, rather than disclosing the analogous experience of the Divine as "lordly" (*Adonai*), near to us (*Shechinah*), and inhering in us and between us as spirit (*Ruah*).

One can speculate, further, that because of the obscurantism of the controversies about transubstantiation over the centuries, my friend would not make a connection between what Christians say of the experience of eating blessed Eucharist bread and drinking Eucharist wine and an observation like Rabbi Heschel's that the Divine may be experienced in so small a thing as "a morsel of bread."[52]

The final problem specific to Jewish-Christian relations I might just call the regular recurrence of recidivist attitudes, the expression of relatively primitive understandings of one another, after much progress and from sources we would least expect. I know this is something that happens among Jews. But relations between Jews and Christians are neither historically nor morally symmetrical. And it is for me, principally, to note instances of backsliding among Christians.

By calling this problem one of recidivism, I am excluding periodic eruptions of naked antisemitism. What I have more in mind is surprising instances when theological anti-Judaism [53] surfaces from unexpected sources. An instructive example is Cardinal Avery Dulles' criticism, in Fall 2002, of the United States Conference of Catholic Bishops' Committee on Ecumenical and Interreligious Affairs' document *Reflections On Covenant and Mission*.

The episcopal document sets out the rationale for the proposition that "targeting Jews for conversion to Christianity...," is "...no longer theologically acceptable in the Catholic Church."[54] In taking exception to this proposition, Dulles manages to sidestep Vatican leaders, papal statements, and the work of the Pontifical Biblical Commission. This highly sophisticated theologian lifts some lines from a polemical text of the New Testament and uses them to demonstrate the permissibility of evangelizing Jews. He does this as if God simply wrote the text, giving voice to God's eternal plan. The text is a portion of the Letter to the Hebrews in which it says that the first covenant is "obsolete" and "ready to vanish away" (Heb 8:13), and that Christ "...abolishes the first...in order to establish the second" (Heb 10:9).

In response to this breakdown of exegesis and to this literalism, three Catholic scholars, with the greatest delicacy, remind this distinguished Catholic theologian (created cardinal by Pope John Paul II precisely to honor his theological work), of actual Vatican theology as well as time-honored theological perspectives on appraising the truth of scriptural texts. They write: "In the words of the Pontifical Biblical Commission 'Interpretation of scripture involves a work of sifting and setting aside....'"[55] And "the magisterium [teaching authority of the church] can explicitly contradict an idea of an individual New Testament author because the Catholic tradition is one of commentary not *sola scriptura* (scripture alone). The author of Hebrews, convinced that he was living in the final stages of history, could argue that the Old Covenant had yielded to the New. Two millennia later, however, in a Church whose pope has prayed for God's forgiveness for the sins of Christians against Jews, such an assertion is unacceptable."[56]

I chose this example because of the deserved prominence of the recidivist and because of the baldness of the actual offense. The response by Mary Boys, Philip Cunningham, and John Pawlikowiski is also instructive in that it is a clear example of the kind of progress made since the achievement of what in chapter two I will call a "second stage" of renewal of relations between Jews and Christians. This is the stage at which, among other examples of progress, polemical anti-Jewish texts of the Second Testament are reinterpreted in the light of the context of the times not taken for timeless divine truth. The point here, in concluding the discussion of special problems associated with deepening Jewish-Christian relations, is that when there can be slippage on matters like this, achieving even more ambitious goals can become remote.

In Praise of Separateness

Nothing proposed here is intended to diminish appreciation of the enrichment of human life by differences, distinctions, even separateness. It is a truism that "variety is the spice of life." The thesis of this book is not built on ignorance of how important separateness is to both the vitality and the survival of the Jewish people (and by extension, any other conceivable pairing of members of religious communities engaged in deep encounter). Therefore a word is in order about the importance of Jewish separateness and distinctiveness in particular as well as about the general value of such separateness or distinctiveness.

David Gelernter gives us a wonderful essay on separateness in Judaism, on how it "governs the Bible's view of how Israel should live among the nations."[57] He writes: "In the beginning, says the Book of Genesis, was chaos—*Tov va 'vohu*—...and chaos means mixed-togetherness, unseparation. To banish chaos, you must separate."[58]

In the Book of Leviticus. God says "Make yourself holy and be holy for I am holy" (Lev 11:44). But in a midrash (rabbinic commentary) on the verse, God's words are changed to "As I am separate, so you be separate."[59] And in the Zohar, the great late thirteenth-century mystical tract of Moses de Leon, it is said "Happy are Israel...the Holy One, Blessed be He, has separated them from all other nations."[60]

The precursors of rabbinic Judaism, the Pharisees, take their name from the Hebrew—*perushim*—for "the separate ones."[61]

Creation itself consists of separation of earth, sea, and land, and liberation (exodus), of the separation of the Red Sea. Light is separate from darkness, day from night, breeds of animals and seeds from one another. So too are men from women, betrothed women from other men, Jews from Canaanites, milk from meat and the Sabbath from *havdalah*, the "separation blessing" that brings Sabbath to a close.

Gelernter moves compellingly from the symbolic to the sociological. He says that separation from Germany in the 1930s required of German Jews "the enormously painful step of separating themselves from their native world." And that "American Jews are asked to take a vastly smaller step of separation...when they are requested to disapprove of their sons and daughters marrying gentiles."[62] What is at stake is clear and moving: "In human society...a people disperses—mixes with other people and gets lost like a teardrop in the ocean."[63]

But Judaism is against dispersal, or should be. And "each time [a Jew] makes a separation or looks through a separation or marches into a separation, he shouts out loud his defiance of chaos...and death." [64]

So separateness is a deeply compelling issue for Jews. As Gelernter says, Jews and their persecutors through history have "collaborated" in Jewish separateness. Separateness has led Jews and Judaism to extraordinary heights of human achievement, and it has made them objects of scorn. The ultimate importance of an appropriate degree of separateness, of distinctiveness, for the Jewish people is that they shall not disappear; they must not become teardrops in the ocean. But distinctiveness or separateness is a universal value, what Heschel calls "the sense of the unique."[65] He writes eloquently of this yearning for distinctiveness expressed on the individual plane: "To the world I am an ordinary man. But to myself I am not ordinary. The issue becomes how to actualize the quiet eminence of my own being."[66]

In a universal key, we celebrate the relationship between separateness, or separation, and holiness. In a religious context, we would say holiness is the concrete process of being saved where salvation is understood not in cosmic and mythological terms but existentially. John Hicks speaks this way calling salvation "an actual human change, a gradual transformation from natural self-centeredness...to a radical new orientation centered in God and manifested in the 'fruits of the Spirit.'"[67]

It dramatizes the link between holiness in this sense and the need for separation and distinction if we consider a contemplative model of holiness. In this mode, every human strength we would strive to cultivate requires separation and even periodic retreat from the larger prevailing influence of our culture. One seeks to grow still surrounded by noise, simple in front of ravenous consumption, slow when everyone is being fast. The goal is gentleness in a sea of violence and calm reflectiveness where many are dispersed and scattered.

Separateness, in so far as it is the necessary condition for the preservation of some distinctiveness, is intrinsic to every healthy religious community and spiritual way. As my teacher, Gabriel Moran, has never ceased to insist (chiefly because over the years the importance he attaches to the distinction between "religion" and "religiousness" has been so often misunderstood), there is no religion in general. There are only specific communities in which specific symbols, rituals, convictions, moral practices, and patterns of common life are effective in promoting lives of holiness, lives in which the divine-human relationship is experienced, the practice of justice, forgiveness, and compassion endorsed, and people in some significant numbers helped to live well and happily. It must be that this value, legitimate separateness, can co-exist with deepening encounter of people in different religious communities.

Spiritual Companionship

The risks of working toward a deeper level of encounter between people in different religious communities are hardly greater than those of an inappropriate segregation or isolation from each other. As Heschel says, we really need each other to search together in the wilderness for devotion, for stillness, for love and care, for the courage to believe, for a resurrection of sensitivity and a revival of conscience. We need clues from one another, beyond the patterns of any one religious community, clues which may correct or complement the perspectives and practices prominent in our own religious communities.

Here we return to the earlier discussion of Paul Knitter's distinction between the idea that all religions have the same essential task and the view that each has a different task. The latter idea, which Knitter associates with John Cobb, was also championed by Bede Griffiths. In *Return to the Center*, Griffiths proposes that the great Middle Eastern religions promote a sense and taste for the transcendent and the Eastern religions for immanence. Regardless of how one views the issue, the potential for clues from one religious community and spiritual way enriching others remains. For ultimately, growth from spiritual companionship is entirely existential. By existential I mean compelling, concrete, real, and immediate, affecting me now.

I have shared how, concretely and really, Jews and Judaism help me retrieve and celebrate the incarnational ethos: that the divine and human are locked in intimate embrace. This is an inheritance of my Catholic upbringing, but somewhat muted by the Jansenistic (moralistic) tinge of that mid-twentieth century "Irish (American) Catholicism." In the same way, the wedding of Zen practice with Christian prayer of silence is an indispensable strength in my life. On these experiences, and others, rests my claim that "each and every religious community should sponsor interreligious encounter of this kind." I think these are precisely the kind and quality of human experiences to which Bernard Lonergan was referring when he said that "it is through knowledge and appreciation of others that we come to know ourselves and to fill out and refine our appreciation of values."[68]

And we should be clear about the outcomes we seek, about what truly enriches. We will know encounters leading to spiritual companionship are succeeding if these encounters hasten and deepen the qualities of faithfulness in those engaged in the encounters. The faithfulness is to the human vocation. The human vocation is to practice becoming a masterpiece. To practice becoming a masterpiece is to practice living well. To live well is to grow, perhaps only little by little, in the qualities of reverence, gratefulness, joy, stillness (or silence), creativity, courage, justice, forgiveness, compassion, and (in a religious context), praise and penitence before the Holy One.

If it true that this work of faithfulness can be enhanced by sponsoring encounter beyond dialogue (though not in opposition to it), it would be a shame if such encounter were thwarted for fear of relativizing truth claims. Here we return to David Novak's claim "that some things are true all the time, everywhere and for everyone...." This is a formula for concluding dialogue before it can advance to deeper levels of encounter, even spiritual companionship. It is also quite simply not so. There is, however, *one thing* that is true all the time. It is a truth that might be experienced and celebrated by *everyone, everywhere.* And this one thing, in the words of Jacques Dupuis, is that "the principle agent of interreligious dialogue is the Spirit of God, who is present in the traditions on both sides and who animates the partners.... It is the same God who works saving deeds in human history and who speaks to human beings in the depths of their hearts."[69]

The next chapter explores the evolution of relations between Jews and Christians to the brink of spiritual companionship. It contains a fuller treatment of the problems surrounding this evolution, and it frames in an introductory way ideas dealt with in subsequent chapters. Chapter three deals with the pivotal theological issue of revelation; chapter four with what I have already referred to as "the usefulness of Christian beliefs to Jewish companions." The final chapter, chapter five, deals with the essential practice for achieving spiritual companionship, the practice of contemplation. And the epilogue deals with how we teach one another about one another.

What is before us is how to find a path for people in any two religious communities (Jews and Christians are employed as an example), a path beyond fixation on truth claims, a path to deepened spiritual lives, and therefore, a path to enhanced practice of justice, forgiveness and compassion.

I think Irving (Yitz) Greenberg (not alone but profoundly) understands that this is the proper path and how to travel it. Greenberg seems to stake faithfulness itself on the quality of the encounter. He writes that the very authenticity of Jewish embrace of the covenant "will demand that Jews and Christians remain open to each other, that we learn from each other."[70] He affirms that there must be "respect for the distinctiveness and validity of each other's traditions."[71] But, unlike Novak, Greenberg acknowledges that "Such openness puts no religious claim beyond possibility."[72] And finally he tells us that the affirmation of a deep level of interreligious encounter need do nothing "to undercut the belief of each group that it is *an* [my emphasis] elected people of God. There is enough love in God to choose again and again."[73] These are ideal words with which to continue.

Notes

1. Quoted in Margaret Farley, *Personal Commitments: Beginning, Keeping, and Changing Them* (San Francisco: Harper and Row, 1986), p. 56.

2. Cyprian Consiglio in Bruno Barnhart and Joseph Wong, *Purity of Heart and Contemplation: A Monastic Dialogue Between Christian and Asian Traditions* (New York: Continuum, 2001), p. 67.

3. Galatians 2:19f in the *New Revised Standard Version.*

4. Shunryu Suzuki. *Zen Mind, Beginner's Mind* (New York: Walker/Weatherhill, 1970), p. #1f.

5. Cited in Shaykh Fadhlalla Haeri, *The Elements of Sufism* (Shaftesbury, Dorset, GB: Longmead, 1990), p. 53.

6. Quoted in Barnhart and Wong, op. cit., p. 64.

7. In Jonathan Montaldo and Patrick Hart, OCSO, *The Intimate Merton: His Life from His Journals* (New York: Harper Collins, 1999), p. 86.

8. Thomas Merton, *Thoughts in Solitude* (New York: Farrar, Strauss and Giroux, 1956), p. 46.

9. Raimundo Panikkar, *The Intrareligious Dialogue* (San Francisco: Harper and Row, 1978), p. xxvii.

10. Quoted from "De Mutatione Nominum," David Winston, translator, in *Philo of Alexandria: The Contemplative Life, The Giants and Selections.* (New York: Paulist Press, 1981), p. 233.

11. Conrad Hyers, *The Comic Vision and the Christian Faith: A Celebration of Life and Laughter* (New York: Pilgrim Press, 1981), p. 35.

12. David Tracy, "The Christian Understanding of Salvation-Liberation," *Face to Face: An Interreligious Bulletin*, vol. XIV, 1988, pp 40–44. "The move to total liberation in these Christian interpretations of 'salvation' is...correctly described as a necessary re-Judaizing of Christian soteriology against some individualistic, ahistorical and apolitical traditional readings."

13. I summarized these impressions in chapter five, "The Genius of Judaism," Padraic O'Hare, *The Enduring Covenant: The Education of Christians and the End of Antisemitism* (Valley Forge, PA: Trinity Press International, 1997), pp. 128–151.

14. In Samuel Dresner (ed), *I Asked For Wonder: A Spiritual Anthology of Abraham Joshua Heschel* (New York: Crossroad Press, 1997), p. 46.

15. This is a generative theme running throughout the rich, broad, and deep work of many decades, of my teacher, Gabriel Moran.

16. Roger Haight, SJ, *Jesus, Symbol of God* (Maryknoll, NY: Orbis Press, 2000), p. 194.

17. Quoted in Reinhold Niebuhr, *The Nature and Destiny of Man*, vol. 1, (New York: Scribner, 1956), p. 157.

18. Padraic O'Hare, *The Way of Faithfulness: Contemplation and Formation in the Church* (Valley Forge, PA: Trinity Press International, 1993), and *Busy Life, Peaceful Center: A Book of Meditating* (Chicago: Thomas More Press, 1995).

19. Quoted in Frank Ephrain Talmadge (ed.), *Disputation and Dialogue: Readings of Jewish-Christian Encounter* (New York: KTAV Publishing House and the Anti-Defamation League, 1975), p. 86.

20. Leonard Swidler, *After the Absolute: The Dialogical Future of Religious Reflection* (Minneapolis: Fortress Press, 1990), p. 52.

21. An excellent example of embodying of both the limitations of the "dialogue" model and its incipient possibilities is Tikva Frrymer-Kensky, David Novak, et al (eds), *Christianity in Jewish Terms* (Boulder, CO: Westview Press, 2000).

22. Ibid. p. 4

23. In Talmadge. op.cit., p. 348.

24. In *The Praktikos* (Kalamazoo, MI: Cisterian Publications, 1978), p. 65. Translated with an Introduction by John Eudes Bamberger, OCSO.

25. Abraham Joshua Heschel, *The Insecurities of Freedom* (New York: Farrar, Straus and Giroux, 1966), p.112ff.

26. Mary C. Boys, *Has God Only One Blessing? Judaism as a Source of Christian Self-Understanding* (New York: Paulist Press, 2000), p. 271.

27. Krister Stendahl, "Fom God's Perspective We Are All Minorities," *Journal of Religious Pluralism*, 1993, p. 10.

28. David Ellenson quoted in Boys, op. cit. p. 277f.
29. David Tracy, *Blessed Rage For Order: The New Pluralism in Theology* (New York: Seabury Press, 1975), p. 4.
30. Boys. op. cit. p. 277.
31. Quoted in Mary Boys and Sara Lee, "The Catholic-Jewish Colloquium: An Experiment in Interreligious Learning," *Religious Education*, vol. 91, no. 4. 1996, p. 432.
32. Susannah Heschel (ed), *Moral Grandeur and Spiritual Audacity* (New York: Farrar, Straus and Giroux, 1996) p. 402.
33. Padraic O'Hare, *The Enduring Covenant*, op.cit., p. 57f.
34. Paul Knitter (ed), *Transforming Christianity and the World: A Way Beyond Absolutism and Relativism* (Maryknoll, NY: Orbis Press, 1999), p. 61.
35. Ibid.
36. Martin Marty and R. Scott Appleby, *Accounting For Fundamentalism* (Chicago: University of Chicago Press, 1992), p. 1.
37. Patrick Arnold, SJ, "The Rise of Catholic Fundamentalism," *America*, April 11, 1987, p. 298.
38. Pope John Paul II,"For Pontiff Day of Emotion," *Boston Globe*, August 19, 2002, p. A8.
39. Pope John Paul II, *Crossing the Threshold of Hope* (New York: Alfred A. Knopf, 1994), p. 85ff. The Pope speaks in part well of Buddhism, but ultimately as a system of a "purely negative enlightenment" in which the world is seen as bad.
40. Cited in "Zen and the Impurity of Purity" by Francis H. Cook, Barnhart and Wong. op cit. p. 124. See also Leo D. Lefebure "Cardinal Ratzinger's Comments On Buddhism," *Buddhist Christian Studies*, 18 (1998) 221–223.
41. Ibid.
42. Ibid., p. 124f.
43. In Austin Flannery OP (ed), *The Basic Sixteen Documents of Vatican Council II* (Northport, NY: Costello Publishing Company, 1996), p. 469.
44. See note 12 above.
45. David D. Kertzer, *The Popes Against the Jews: The Vatican's Role in the Rise of Anti-Semitism* (New York: Alfred A. Knopf, 2001).

46. Quoted in Tikva Frymer-Kensky, Novak et al., op. cit. p. XVII. "Dabru Emet means 'to speak the truth.'"

47. Michael S. Kogan, "Christian-Jewish Dialogue in the Twenty-First Century: Where Do We Go From Here? A Jewish Reflection," Conference paper delivered at Boston College, June 18/19, 2000, p. 6.

48. Cited in Mary C. Boys, Philip Cunningham, and John Pawlikowski, SM, "Theology's Sacred Obligation," *America*, Oct. 21, 2002, p. 15. See also Eugene Fischer and Leon Klenecki, eds., *Spiritual Pilgrimage: Texts on Jews and Judaism*, 1979-1995 Pope John Paul II, (Mahwah, NJ: Paulist Press, 1996).

49. Edward Schillbeeckx, OP, *A Survey of Catholic Theology 1800 to 1970*, p. 31. Edited with an introduction by Mark Schcof, OP.

50. John Macquarrie, *Principles of Christian Theology* (New York: Charles Scribner's Sons, 1966), p. 276.

51. Karl Rahner, *Foundations of Theology* (New York: Crossroad, 1985), pp 134–36.

52. In Dresner, op.cit., p. 16.

53. Here the term "anti-Judaism" and the reality behind it is distinguished from antisemitism, the former, to simplify, theological opposition to Jews and Judaism, the latter hating Jews and Judaism. I have dealt at length with the distinction in my 1997 book, *The Enduring Covenant*, see note 13 above. David Kertzer has made a persuasive case that the distinction is vacuous. See note 45 above.

54. Boys, Cunningham, Pawlikowski. op. cit., p. 14.

55. Ibid.

56. Ibid., p. 15.

57. David Gelernter, "Judaism Beyond Words," *Commentary*, vol. 113 #5, May 2002. All quotes from pp. 31–36. My special thanks to Lawrence Lowenthal for bringing this power and thoughtful essay to my attention.

58. Ibid.

59. Ibid.

60. Ibid.

61. Ibid.

62. Ibid.

63. Ibid.

64. Ibid.

65. S. Heschel. op. cit. p. 396.

66. Abraham Joshua Heschel, *Who Is Man?* (Stanford, CA: Stanford University Press, 1965), p. 35.

67. John Hicks "A Pluralist View," in Denis I, Okholm and Timothy R. Philips (eds), *More Than One Way? Four Views on Salvation in a Pluralist World* (Grand Rapids, MI: Zondervan Publishing House), p. 39.

68. Bernard Lonergan, *Method in Theology* (New York: Herder and Herder, 1972), p. 253.

69. Quoted in Barnhart and Wong. op. cit., p. 124.

70. Irving Greenberg "Judaism, Christianity, and Partnership After the Twentieth Century" in Tikva Frymer-Kensky, Novak, et al., op. cit, p. 36.

71. Ibid.

72. Ibid.

73. Ibid.

CHAPTER TWO

What Is Achieved, What Remains

Drawing the Lines in Relations

Two distinguished religious leaders, one Jewish, one Catholic, made a joint presentation in the early months of 2000 to participants in an annual conference for pastoral leaders in Jewish, Catholic, Orthodox Christian, and Protestant congregations from the area in which the conference was held. Their topic was "Jewish-Christian Relations in the Twenty-first Century."

The speakers share deep erudition, genuine commitment to mutual respect between members of varying religious communities, and a focus on how these communities can continue and expand cooperation around issues of mutual ethical concern, minimizing without ignoring disagreements on the moral bases of public policy while influencing such policy for the common good.

Their presentations were crisp, thoughtful, and dwelled on the heartening progress of relations between Jews and Christians. Both emphasized the importance of Jews and Catholics asserting their distinctiveness, the power of their respective symbols, rituals, convictions, moral practices, and patterns of common life. Both linked Jews and Christians making a real contribution to "repair the world" (*Tikkun Olam*) to their unself-conscious celebration of their particularity, their legitimate separateness.

In the discussion between the two after their presentations occasioned by responses to questions and observations from audience members, the follow exchange took place. The Jewish presenter addressed the Catholic on the matter of the delicate balance between members of different religious communities providing mutual and loving correction of one another on the one hand, and lapsing, on the other, into interference in matters strictly internal to each religious community. To paraphrase, what the Jewish leader said went something like this: "I need to challenge you (that is, we need to challenge one another), never to bring the name of God into disrepute; but as to a matter such as the canonization of Pope Pius XII, I have nothing to say to you, no right to interfere in a strictly Catholic matter." The Catholic leader nodded approval.

The tradition to which the Jewish leader made reference is that of "Kiddush Hashem" and "Hillul Hashem": "The one means that everything within one's power should be done to glorify the name of God before the world; the other that everything should be avoided that reflects dishonor on the religion and thereby desecrates the name of God."[1]

For me, as a Catholic for whom the canonization of Pius XII would qualify as compromising these principles, the moment was clarifying. I couldn't know at that point that the even more egregious act of beatifying Pope Pius IX and linking it to the beatification of a genuine hero of Catholic Church reform, Pope John XXIII, would make the talk of Pius XII's cause for canonization seem less problematic by comparison.[2]

In many ways the two men in this story embody the current consensus about what relations between Jews and Christians should and should not be, where they should go and where they should not go. Each of these men associates the vitality of his religious community with retrieving and living a restored Judaism and a restored Catholicism. Both, in other words, are "orthodox," the one a modern orthodox Jew, the other occupying the equivalent terrain, what David

Tracy identifies as a Christian "neo-orthodoxy." Tracy's description covers positions in both communities. The modern orthodox Jew and the neo-orthodox Catholic eschew fundamentalism and focus strategically on the existential vitality of lived practice within the religions. Both express utter assurance about the timeless and exclusive truth and universal efficacy of the symbols, rituals, convictions, moral practices and patterns of common life held and interpreted by conservative synagogue and church members and leadership. [3]

Both emphasize that precious Jewish and Christian religious and moral values are besieged and marginal in contemporary secular society, and that vital witness is needed in the face of what Stephen Carter calls "the culture of disbelief." [4] Both would agree with Rabbi Heschel writing in the 1960s: "What do we claim? That religious commitment is not just an ingredient of the social order, an adjunct or reinforcement of existence, but rather the heart and core of being human." [5]

Both men would, however, be readier than Heschel to associate the diminished role of religious commitment with theological liberalism, to criticize the liberal impulse and to associate it with a too-intimate engagement of religious communities with one another likely to lead to relativism. Heschel, after all, while insisting on separateness [6], was breathtaking in his repudiation of exclusive claims to divine preference as well as in his regular and strong indictment of moral timidity in the leaders of religious institutions.

I need to leave these two estimable leaders and men be. Their positions are defensible, the good they do palpable. I have no dispute with them since I seek in this book to follow Cardinal Newman's injunction to prefer inquiry to dispute. My inquiry, however, will lead well beyond the model of relations that they embody.

Before leaving them, however, it would be instructive to identify their models and patrons, the teachers in whose debt they stand, teachers who are explicitly invoked by them. The larger-than-life figures who define the present richness as well as the broadly held view of the limits on further evolution of relations between Jews and Christians (or certainly Catholics) are Pope John Paul II and Rabbi Joseph Soloveitchick (both now deceased). Considering the ambiguity of Pope John Paul's place in Jewish-Christian relations and the breathtaking clarity of Rabbi Soloveitchick's insistence on the limits of these relations helps us frame advocacy for the further and future evolution of these same relations, an evolution through deep spiritual encounter to spiritual companionship.

Wojtyla and Soloveitchick

In the light, quite literally the luminescence, of Pope John Paul's profoundly moving, heartfelt and reconciling visit to Israel in March 2000, one hesitates to identify his role as ambiguous. Who can fail to be touched by his words at Yad Vashem: "Here, as at Auschwitz and many other places...we are overcome by the heart-rending laments of so many. Men, women, children cry out to us from the depths of the horror that they knew. How can we fail to hear their cry....As Bishop of Rome and successor of the Apostle Peter, I assure the Jewish people that the Catholic Church...is deeply saddened by the hatred, acts of persecution and displays of anti-Semitism directed against Jews by Christians at any time and in any place"[7]

This historical occasion is but the highpoint of a pontificate-long evolution of decisive acts designed to further reconciliation between Jews and Catholics: the 1985 Vatican guidelines for the proper teaching about Jews and Judaism, the papal visit to Auschwitz, the pope's 1986 visit to the Roman synagogue and embrace of the chief rabbi, Elio Toaff. (Until the image of the pope at the Western Wall the depiction of this embrace was, perhaps, history's most telling and expressive icon of reconciliation between religions.) And there is the commemoration of the Shoah at the Vatican and diplomatic recognition of the State of Israel, both acts of great care and of healing.

Nevertheless, ambiguity, or paradox, abounds. At one level, the ambiguity takes the form of regular backward steps, and profound ones at that, mixed with progress in Vatican initiatives in the realm of Jewish-Christian relations. The 1993 *Catechism of the Catholic Church*, a global Catholic teaching instrument in which restorationist ecclesiastical leaders invest so much hope, is at once silent about the Shoah, recidivist in the language it employs to frame the character and relationship of the Jewish and Christian covenants, and archaic in recapitulating classical language of the doctrine of Christ and of soteriology (the work of Christ in salvation).[8] The long-awaited 1998 document on the Church's role during the Shoah is at least disappointing if not cynical in distinguishing an apparently sinless Church from erring Catholics and in affording the defense of Pope Pius XII a central place in the text.

Commenting on the latter, Garry Wills writes: "Commiserating with victims who lost their lives has to pause while the document takes time to defend the victim [Pius]—a thing that might more properly have been undertaken elsewhere since Pius, though perhaps a defensible figure, is hardly an ecumenical one."[9] Ambiguity turns to contradiction and backpedaling with the publication in September 2000 by the Congregation for the Doctrine of the Faith of Dominus Iesus, with its identification of "interreligious dialogue" with the Church's "evangelizing mission" and its flirtation with the discredited teaching that outside the Church there is no salvation under the guise of reasserting what needs no reassertion: that to be a Christian is to experience and proclaim Jesus Christ as one's Lord.

Finally there is the disconcerting rash of politics of canonization throughout the 1990s which has entailed the canonization of Edith Stein as a martyr for the faith, of Maximilian Kolbe without regard to his association with virulent streams of Polish Catholic antisemitism, and the movement to eventually canonize Pope Pius XII to which is added the beatification of the reactionary Pius IX, the kidnapper of Edgardo Montaro.[10]

A deeper and more troublesome level of ambiguity or paradox exists in the contradiction between the evolution of empathy between Catholics and Jews and the dismantling, during Pope John Paul's restorationist papacy, of the bracing range of conciliar reforms set in motion by Pope John XXIII and moved forward by Pope Paul VI at the Second Vatican Council (1962-65) and through much of the 1970s. In broad general terms, the conciliar reform of the Catholic Church set it on a course that should lead to a religious community which is:

1. *Thoroughly pastoral*, which is to say one in which the practice of the Church is unwaveringly designed to nurture and support people to live holy lives.

2. *Intellectually honest*, in which the function of theological reflection at all levels is free and open to what was called during the Council "the signs of the times," an openness inspired by the Holy Spirit to correct and purify Church teaching and practice so that it grows ever more pastoral.

3. *Ecclesiologically horizontal*, which is to say a Church more fully understanding itself as a people of God.

4. *Increasingly collegial*, in which all the people of the Church and beyond the Church are viewed as potential sources of inspiration for its continuing enhancement, its purification.

5. *Profoundly celebratory*, in which worship (for Catholics especially an experience of "one-ing," or *henosis*, with Christ and one another in the Eucharist and for Protestants in the preached word),[11] is the singular mark of the community and, more generally, in which the happiness of members of the community—the inheritance of their "original blessing" in Matthew Fox's phrase—is the means and end of the community's moral discourse and practice.

6. *Continually developing*, which is to say, with Cardinal Newman, that the "convictional" or intellectual element of faithfulness is ever more adequately formulated.

7. *More profoundly inclusive*, with men and women, ordained and lay, gay and straight, a broad range of human experiences and variety of persons heard in the circle in which the pastoral efficacy of Church practice is determined and carried on.

8. Above all, *the Christ of conciliar Catholicism* is not so much the triumphal king, the sign of whose cross is so often and readily employed to bolster ecclesiastical power, nor the necessary victim for satisfying the wrath of an offended God. The Christ of conciliar Catholicism is he who is encountered deeply in Eucharist and word, with whom Christians die and rise and are flooded with compassion (and compunction), experience profound gratitude for ordinary things and oneness with the Holy One. This Christ, to

borrow a phrase of Nietzsche's, is a "monumental event" encountered again and again if only fleetingly in the actual existential depths of the Christian's life.

In contrast to the conciliar reforms, Pope John Paul's restorationist papacy has promoted:

1. A return to the juridical model of the Church with sure criteria of membership found in conformity, really selective conformity, to ecclesiastical rule.

2. A repressing of theological discourse, which leads Garry Wills to observe: "The arguments for what passes as current Church doctrine are so intellectually contemptible that mere self-respect forbids a man to voice them as his own."[12]

3. An effort to return to a model of the Church as composed of *ecclesia docens* and *discens*, the "Church teaching and the Church taught," a model ensuring that only a small swath of human experience is present in ecclesiastical councils.

4. The reassertion of an autocratic structure of the Church, which is not in conformity with earliest traditions and contradicts the biblical idea of gifts of the Holy Spirit.

5. A reassertion of the primacy of dogma as the hallmark of the belonging Catholic, a return to seeing *orthodoxis* (right belief) as superior to *orthopraxis* (right action).[13]

6. As the term "restoration" denotes, a greater interest in returning than in developing and not returning very far back but only so far as necessary to assert specious historical claims for an autocracy in papacy and episcopacy.

7. Exclusion, of laity from a domain of clerical initiative, women from a domain of male initiative, the marginalization of Catholics who are gay and lesbian, an exclusionary strategy that returns us to moral rigorism after the brief experiment of the conciliar embrace of positive moral theology.

8. Above all, a return to Christ the King, sympathetically and intimately related to his vicar on earth and identified chiefly with the Catholic Church and not with other Christian ecclesial communities.

What has this to do with Jewish-Christian relations and their evolution to a stage of spiritual companionship? What has it to do with going further and deeper in our relations? Everything. This is not a litany of intramural matters about which Jews should have nothing to say to Catholics or with which Catholics focused on these relations need not be concerned. Pope John XXIII's church headed away from triumphalism; Pope John Paul II's church headed well down the road to its restoration, and this despite remarkable ecumenical gestures as well as substance such as the prayer at Assisi, the Jubilee round of apologies, and the like. Every feature of the restoration sketched here crimps the range of human experience, diversity, and insight available in ecclesial counsels and renders prejudice more likely. Every feature of the restoration is defensive and nourishes a kind of tribal Vatican reaction seen in such wagon-circling words as: "What more do the Jews want?"[14] If the goal is "return," and it so obviously is, to what is official Catholicism returning? What marks our history with Jews, with Muslims?

Christian triumphalism is ecclesiological and eschatological. Ecclesiological triumphalism makes claims for the Church and the escatological kind makes claims about the "end times." (As a former theology professor of mine loved to roll off his lips threateningly "death, judgment, heaven and [or] hell".)

Ecclesiological triumphalism claims absolute correspondence between dogmatic and disciplinary pronouncements of church officials and reality itself. It ascribes inerrancy to a broad range of teachings and actions of these officials.

Eschatological triumphalism is related to the ecclesiological type since it claims exclusive dispensation of salvation by the Church. It was effectively repudiated at the Second Vatican Council in documents such as the *Declaration on Religious Freedom* and especially in the teaching in the *Constitution on the Church's Relations with the Non-Christian Religions* (*Nostra Aetate*) which, for example, citing Saint Paul, states that "...the Jews remain very dear to God...since God does not take back the gifts He bestowed or the choice he made."[15]

But that was 1965. In the year 2000, we had the recidivist document from the Congregation for the Doctrine of the Faith, *Dominus Iesus*, to which reference was made earlier. And the 1993 *Catechism of the Catholic Church* states: "The Church does not know any means other than baptism that assures entry into eternal beatitude; this is why she takes care not to neglect the mission she has received from the Lord to see that all who can be baptized are 'reborn of water and the Holy Spirit.' God has bound salvation to the sacrament of baptism, but he himself [reassuring?] is not bound by his sacraments.'"[16]

Deeper encounter, even to spiritual companionship, requires that all such triumphalism end. And this requires personal and institutional humility. We noted this in chapter one while contrasting David Novak's view of the status of religious truth claims with those of Rabbi Heschel. The full text of the Heschel quote is this: "I suggest that the most significant basis for meeting of men of different religious traditions, is the level of fear and trembling, of humility and contrition, where our individual moments of faith are mere waves in the ocean of mankind's reaching out for God, where all formulations and articulations appear as understatements, where our souls are swept away by the awareness of the urgency of answering God's commandments, while stripped of pretension and conceit we sense the tragic insufficiency of human faith."[17]

James Carroll holds a compelling view of the contradiction between deepened encounter and triumphal claims. He writes "That John Paul II has reasserted the idea of infallibility, on the one hand, while demonstrating an unprecedented and genuine sympathy for Jews on the other, is the great paradox of his papacy. And it could yet become his tragedy, for what is needed, after Auschwitz, is an adjustment in attitudes not toward Jews but toward the claims the Church makes on the soul of the world. Jews are, in a very real sense, the original and quintessential dissenters from that claim: Judaism calls into question the supremacist universalism of Christology."[18]

Pope John Paul's position was ambiguous and in part contradictory. No such ambiguity attaches to Rabbi Joseph Soloveitchick's view of relations, nor I think is his position in any substantive sense triumphal.

Soloveitchick was "perhaps the most famous Orthodox Jewish proponent of Jewish-Christian dialogue...."[19] He addressed the appropriate extent and limits of these relations in his 1964 essay

"Confrontation." "Arguing, he claims, from a biblical perspective, Soloveitchick asserts that confrontation is the essence of human life."[20] The confrontation is with both the world and with human beings. Randi Rashkover characterizes Soloveitchick's position in this way: "Jews must participate in both types of confrontation, and yet it is only in the confrontation with nature where we [Jews] can meet with non-Jews in a common conversation about efforts to control our world and our resources. The curtain of conversation falls when we engage as Jews in the confrontation unique to our covenant community."[21] Soloveitchick himself writes: "It is important that the religious or theological logos should not be employed as the medium of communication between two faith communities....The conversation should not occur at a theological but at a mundane human level....Our common interests lie not in the realm of faith but in that of the secular orders."[22]

Problems of the Next Stages: I

The response of the Catholic (an approving nod) as well as the initial delimitation made by the Jew in the anecdote with which this chapter opened make clear, I think, that mainstream proponents, both Jewish and Christian, of enhanced relations nevertheless believe a "curtain of conversation" must fall when the "realm of faith" is approached. But motives vary at least up to a point. As I noted in chapter one, the history of Jewish survival, linked as it is in part but significantly to separateness, as well as perennial Jewish minority status, provide powerful social and historical motives for caution even among Jews for whom theological dialogue is highly prized. And again, the history of the "teaching of contempt,"[23] the centuries of anti-Jewish Christian Replacement theology (supersessionism, literally "to sit above," the idea that the Christians have replaced the Jews in God's affections), this history and its tragic consequences for Jews, all this can sharpen caution to a point where it may be near impossible for many Jews to embrace the further evolution of relations envisioned in this book.

The dominant motive of Christian advocates of good relations, who nevertheless draw a curtain in the realm of faith, is surely theological. No theological position exists outside a social context, and certainly the majority status of Christianity throughout much of the last two millennia in the West is a factor in the theological assertion of a christological doctrine that is universalistic even when it is inclusive. (Only Jesus Christ is savior, but all may be saved in his name).[24] The renewed triumphalism of the restorationist papacy plays an important part in framing the present consensus on the limits of relations. But one need not posit the "extra *ecclesia nulla salus*...," [outside the church no salvation] of imperial Catholicism, or for that matter an ultra-Orthodox Jewish interpretation of the meaning of chosenness, to understand either the social and historical or the theological grounds for reluctance to see the lines of separateness of religious communities become more permeable. Socially, such reluctance lies in an appreciation of what constitutes groups, a commonsensical insight about the relationship between identity, belonging, and separation which was addressed in chapter one.

Still, where theological reasons are in play, resistance to seeing relations evolve to deeper encounter rests on fear that a unique revelation will be lost in relativism and syncretism (the destructive mixing of elements of religions). To use Robley Whitson's phrase, it is fear of the "coming convergence of world religions."[25]

In addition to these theological and sociological reasons, and ironically, the very progress of Jewish-Christian relations in the past fifty years may also block deeper encounter. These relations have improved dramatically; James Carroll makes this case clearly. Criticized by restorationist Catholics for the courageousness and consistency with which he links ecclesiastical triumphalism to the perennial possibility of renewed antisemitism, Carroll nevertheless makes this telling point about the genuineness of official Catholic overtures to the Jewish people: for all the occasional backsliding, in our time the worldwide leadership in the Vatican of approximately one billion Catholics cares deeply about what a people numbering around fourteen million thinks and feels.

Carroll's position among those who care deeply about Jewish-Christian relations is precisely my own. The way he links the hubris and authoritarianism of official Catholicism with the possible resurgence of anti-Judaism and antisemitism, even amidst the celebration of our repaired relations, seems to offend mainstream Christians as much as it does full-bore triumphalists. His 1997 essay in *The New Yorker* treating this topic[26] was subject to a scathing rejoinder in the well-regarded moderate journal of mostly Catholic opinion, *Commonweal*. There, Paul Bauman was moved to ask: "Has it occurred to Carroll that his itch to 'de-absolutize' religion is incompatible with monotheism?"[27] This astounding claim dramatizes the difficulty of deepening relations. For it is, of course, precisely in de-absolutizing religion that monotheism is preserved. Witness great Catholic, Protestant, and Jewish theologians addressing the very point: "Something [new] is possible because something [new] *must* (his emphasis) be possible if it is a matter of the inexhaustible riches of God's presence with us....Every formula transcends itself...not because it is false but because it is true" (Karl Rahner).[28] "In the depths of every living religion...that to which it points breaks through its particularity, elevating it to a spiritual freedom and with it to a vision of the spiritual presence in other expressions of the ultimate meaning of man's existence" (Paul Tillich).[29] "God is greater than religion; faith is greater than dogma" (Abraham J. Heschel).[30]

The Next Stage

I leave it to the reader to decide whether what was proposed in chapter one and is being put in context in this chapter is a step to a new stage or a leap into a new paradigm. I have spoken of an evolution beyond theological dialogue and of a "mainstream" perspective in Jewish-Christian relations. I have also pointed to figures, both anonymous and world famous, who embody the mainstream. The substance of the mainstream requires further explanation. One way to do this is to consider the stages at which we have already arrived.

The Shoah, a stage of Christian remorse for the ways in which the centuries of the "teaching of contempt" predisposed Christians to be complicitous, as perpetrators or bystanders, in the genocide of the Jews of Europe, led to profound change in how Christian theology and official ecclesial policy statements spoke of Jews and Judaism. Popular attitudes change slowly, however, and examples still exist of utterly unregenerate anti-Semitism masked in Christian rhetoric, as well as the comparatively more benign anti-Jewish theological backsliding to which reference was made earlier. Nevertheless, since the middle of the last century there has been dramatic improvement. In *Has God Only One Blessing? Judaism As a Source of Christian Self-Understanding*, Mary Boys identifies "...six themes that can be discerned in the Protestant and Catholic reevaluation":

1. refutation of the charge of decide

2. repudiation of antisemitism

3. repentance in regard to the Shoah

4. rejection of proselytizing

5. review of teaching about Jews and Judaism

6. recognition of Israel.

Boys notes, thoughtfully, that the extent of the consensus among Christians trying to repair relations lessens in the case of the latter three elements.[31]

A second overlapping stage, rooted in scholarly work, recognizes the "Jewishness of Jesus" and of the Christian movement, and paints a more accurate, less prejudicial picture of the first century of the common era and of the primitive church. Scholarship clears away historical inaccuracies and textual polemics used to stereotype and calumniate Jews through the centuries. In place of simple dichotomies beholden to these polemical texts in which legalistic Pharisees are contrasted with loving Christians, we have Christian leaders and scholars now speaking in this fashion: "Jesus was perhaps closer to the Pharisees in his religious vision than to any other group of his time....this affinity...may be the reason for many of his apparent controversies with them....Jesus shared with the Pharisees a number of distinctive doctrines: the resurrection of the body; forms of piety such as almsgiving, daily prayer and fasting, the liturgical practice of identifying God as father, and the priority of the love commandment."[32]

A third stage, again overlapping the others, can in a sense be identified with "relations" themselves. Jews and Christians relate to one another more and with greater respect, understanding, affection, and friendship as well as in theological dialogue and pursuit of common moral purposes and practices. Jews and Christians cooperate more, as Rabbi Solveitchick envisioned, to act together to "heal the world."

These stages (perhaps they may be called stages of remorse, scholarship, and collaboration), endure side by side with one another. None of the functions characterizing any one stage are meant to fade away and be replaced. There is suspicion among Jews and Christians at any hint that perhaps the time has come (or will ever come) when historians, theologians, and religious educators can cease attending to the outcomes of the "teaching of contempt."

A story dear to the great ecumenist, pastor, and scripture scholar, Krister Stendahl, reintroduces the emerging stage (the "next stage") in Jewish-Christian relations. Stendahl has often told the story of the rebbe who asked his student "Do you love me?" To which the student replies, "You know I love you, Rebbe!" "Do you know," the rebbe asks, "what makes me happy, what makes me sad?" "No Rebbe," replies the student. "How, then," says the Rebbe, "can you say you love me if you do not know me, if you do not know what makes me happy, what makes me sad?"[33]

Achieving the fourth stage of relations, the stage of spiritual companionship, is really a work of love. For this, for all the peril of the teardrop disappearing in the ocean, the boundaries of our religious communities must grow sufficiently permeable that our ways of faithfulness become transparent to one another, and we become capable of both correcting and forgiving one another.

We have already spoken of some blocks to spiritual companionship. One of these is the traffic in triumphal truth claims. Another is the fallacy that there are two faith communities (or three or a hundred). The yearning for faithfulness is what the Holy One places in every heart; a way of faithfulness, as we've called it, is what we have in common. There are two—there are a hundred—religious communities, but only one way of faithfulness. This distinction, between many religions and one universal yearning for faithfulness, for which I am indebted to my teacher, Gabriel Moran, opens to considering another idea that may help clarify the reality of spiritual companionship and help achieve it. The idea is the difference, though complementary, between religion and spirituality.

Spirituality and Religion

Deep within the institutional expressions of religion there is the spiritual way the religious community seeks to plant and nurture in the hearts and minds, the valuations and practices of confessants. The spiritual ways embedded in religions help members grow in reverence and gratitude, in joy and silence, in creativity and courage, in justice, forgiveness, and compassion, in praise and penitence before God. Above all, the spiritual ways of most religions at their best (but always unevenly) cultivate presence to the Holy One. And presence requires the capacity for stillness, or what Thomas Merton called "interior solitude." Consequently, most religious traditions teach a discipline of contemplation.

Presence is at the heart of all the qualities noted above. Carol Ochs writes of it: "Presence is not simply healing; it is frequently wounding. It satisfies all longing while it creates a longing that cannot be satisfied."[34] And Thomas Merton writes of "prayer in solitude," a principal form of prayer for presence to the Holy One: "...the way of prayer brings us face to face with the sham and indignity of the false self that seeks to live for itself alone."[35] Merton also writes, as noted earlier, that "The spiritual life is first of all a life...first of all a matter of keeping awake. We must not lose our sensitivity to spiritual inspiration....If you want to have a spiritual life you must unify your life. A life is either all spiritual or not spiritual at all. No man can serve two masters. Your life is shaped by the end you live for. You are made in the image of what you desire."[36]

This schooling of desire in the silence of Divine Presence,[37] is crucial to living a faithful life, what Rabbi Heschel calls life as "works of art."[38] This is having a spiritual life! It entails the transformation from living casually to carefully, superficially to significantly, living a life that transcends narrow self-interest and self-absorption.

The religions are fragile instruments for conveying and effecting spiritual living. They specify the spiritual life in distinctive symbols, rituals, convictions, moral practices and pattern of common life. In all their variety and peculiarity, religions are intended to nurture "life-toward-holiness," living a life, little by little, which is commensurate with being a child of God. It is almost too easy, a bit of a cheap shot, to begin to recount the sorry history of the short fall in every religion between spiritual aspirations and religious institutions. Caution is crucial here because it is a good bet that trying to excise a pattern of rich spiritual clues from the historical religious communities and institutions in which they are embedded is almost certain to destroy both.

If spiritual yearning comes from God, religions are human constructs: we make the whole "sacred system." We decide what to make sacred. We impute to religious symbols, rituals, convictions, moral practices, and communal patterns a capacity to lead to the Holy. When such engagement actually leads to more faithful lives, we might say we are in the presence of the "healthy-sacred." Then life within a religious community is instrumental (though not essential) to living a spiritual life.

On the other hand, elements of the sacred system can become ends in themselves apart from the kinds of lives they help form. The elements of the sacred system can be distorted. We might call this the "unhealthy-sacred." When this happens, an ultra-Orthodox Jew invokes God to murder an Israeli prime minister or Muslims at prayer, some Muslims call war holy, some Hindu nationalists slaughter Muslims and Christians, and Christians degrade, humiliate, marginalize, calumnize, and disparage Jews for 2000 years. It is for this reason Rabbi Heschel writes:

> It is an inherent weakness of religion not to take offense at the segregation of God, to forget that the true sanctuary has no walls. Religion has often suffered from the tendency to become an end in itself, to seclude the holy, to become parochial, self-indulgent, self-seeking, as if the task were not to ennoble human nature but to enhance the power and beauty of its institutions or to enlarge the body of doctrine. It has often done more to canonize prejudice than to wrestle for truth; to petrify the sacred than to sanctify the secular.[39]

Spiritual companionship requires that we find ways to engage in spiritual discernment together; ways to evoke the presence of the Holy One together, ways to pray together. Writing of the supreme work of interreligious cooperation, Rabbi Heschel went to the heart of this emerging stage of spiritual companionship, insisting that the culmination and crown of such work is

> to search in the wilderness for wellsprings of devotion, for treasures of stillness, for the power of love and care for man. What is urgently needed is ways of helping one another in the terrible predicament of here and now by the courage to believe that the word of the Lord endures forever as well as here and now; to cooperate in trying to bring about a resurrection of sensitivity, a revival of conscience; to keep alive the divine sparks in our souls, to nurture openness to the spirit of the psalms, reverence for the words of the prophets and faithfulness to the will of God.[40]

Spiritual companionship requires that each of us take seriously the obligations to help one another observe Kiddush Hashem and Hillul Hashem. Against the backdrop of reverence for one another brought about by deepened spiritual encounters, we must cultivate the delicate capacity to correct one another, in love, where the name of the Holy One and the authenticity of the religions' witness to genuine spirituality are at issue. Of this, Ninian Smart writes: "God has created many religions [sic] so that they can keep each other honest! By mutual criticism...they can help to prevent the myopias and corruptions which seem everywhere the concomitants of human worldviews and in particular religious ones."[41] And with specific reference to Christians and Jews, Rabbi Heschel again writes: "Judaism is the mother of the Christian faith. It has a stake in the destiny of Christianity. Should a mother ignore her child...? Is it not our duty to help one another in trying to overcome hardness of heart?"[42]

Problems of the Next Stage: II

It is a marker of just how difficult it is to inaugurate and sustain deepened spiritual encounters that its greatest Jewish proponent, Rabbi Heschel, is accused of theological relativism in proposing something like what is here called spiritual companionship.[43] But such a claim completely misunderstands his crucial distinction between theology and depth theology:

> The theme of theology is the content of believing; the theme of

depth theology is the act of believing....Theology declares, depth theology evokes....Theology demands believing and obedience; depth theology hopes for responding and appreciation. Theology deals with permanent facts; depth theology deals with moments....Theology is like sculpture, depth theology like music. Theology is in books; depth theology is in hearts. The former is doctrine, the latter is events.[44]

The man who said "I would rather go to Auschwitz than give up my religion"[45] was no theological relativist but a prophet and spiritual master who knew, as said earlier, that "God is greater than religion; faith is greater than dogma."[46] That he would be labeled a relativist underscores again the difficulty of achieving what is proposed here.[47]

I noted earlier that one of the problems associated with my proposal is that it calls for heroic new steps in interreligious relations while intramural conflict between fundamentalist and more mainstream elements within Christianity and Judaism (Hinduism, Islam, etc.) escalates.[48]

I also noted the sociological challenge of minority and majority groups shedding to some degree separateness and becoming, as far as possible, transparent to each. But despite these and other problems I am convinced that what Paul Knitter calls "unitive pluralism" must be possible: "Unitive pluralism is a unity in which each religion, although losing some of its individualism (its separate ego), will intensify its personality (its self-awareness through relationship). Each religion will retain its uniqueness but this uniqueness will develop and take on new depth by relating to other religions in mutual dependence."[49]

Another problem of achieving spiritual companionship is the disproportionality of what it calls for from Jews and Christians. This problem was implied in chapter one; it is related to Jewish assimilation and minority status. Setting aside reluctance or resistance based on theological grounds or the memories of Christian-inspired antisemitism, there is also the specter in the United States of what Alan Dershowitz calls "the vanishing American Jew." Intermarriage, assimilation, high percentages of non-observance, demographic contraction, and even the ebbing of overt antisemitism furnish "a new threat to Jewish survival...different from any previously faced."[50] Dershowitz's solution is to launch a renaissance of Jewish religious and spiritual education to serve a people of whom he says: "No group in America is less literate in its language, less familiar with its own library than the Jews. We are the most ignorant, uneducated, illiterate Americans when it comes to knowledge of the Bible, the history of our people, Jewish philosophy, religious rituals and traditions....We get our history from *Fiddler on the Roof*, our traditions from canned gefilte fish, our Bible stories from television, our culture from Jackie Mason, and our Jewish morality from the once-a-year synagogue sermon most of us sleep through."[51]

Even allowing for hyperbole and laugh lines, if Dershowitz has captured something of secularized and assimilated Jews in the United States and Jews living in other modern, consumer societies like it, he is pointing to something that might lead some to resist or postpone an evolution to spiritual companionship in favor of a necessary period of remediation. To cite Gabriel Moran again, just as the call for "teaching to be religious" is sounded, what is perceived as more crucial is "teaching a religion." Teaching to be religious is spiritual education and the recognition of one another as spiritual resources. Teaching a religion is grounding or regrounding a people in the revelatory richness of the symbols, rituals, convictions, moral practices, and patterns of common life of their religious community.

This regrounding or remediation is one of the principal goals of the movement in Judaism called "modern orthodoxy." So it is no surprise that Rabbi Soloveitchick is an inspiration for the movement.

Revelation

The essential theological consideration in this call to a new stage of relations between Jews and Christians (or people in any religious community), is the issue of revelation. In the next chapter, we will take up the issue at length, but some preliminary remarks may be in order here.

If we are siblings, all God's children, and if what the Holy One reveals is a content, a deposit of beliefs, including beliefs about salvific practices, why wouldn't the Holy One give us all the correct name for the Divine, the proper number of sacraments, the inside information on whether hajj is necessary, or circumcision or bathing in the Ganges?

These are, in fact, matters about which the Holy One has as much interest as whether, on a given day, more tangerines or oranges are consumed on the face of the earth! What the Holy One reveals is not a content of belief or practice but God Godself. As Karl Rahner wrote (and this will be explored at length): "Man is the event of the free, unmerited, forgiving and absolute radical self-communication of God."[52]

There is no "content" of revelation which is a simple, unmediated apprehension of the Holy One, no place, in this religion or that, in one dogmatic statement or another, where revelation resides. Revelation is not a deposit kept somewhere or a content of truth claims. Revelation is an experience of a relationship between the Divine and the human which, among other effects, prompts humans to create the sacred.[53] To the extent the sacred elements within a religion nurture faithful people, to that extent these elements (hajj, sacraments, God's name, circumcision, and bathing in the Ganges) should be revered. But the history of brutality in the name of God is largely the result of assigning holiness, virtual identity with God, to what is not holy but only sacred. Edward Robinson's fine book, *Icons of the Present*, is especially helpful in drawing the distinction. Robinson writes of the sacred: "as the means, the door, by which the holy is to be approached; to be celebrated, to be worshiped, even, heaven help us, to be described....The sacred...is always to some degree [sic] a man-made category: a thing, a place, an occasion can all be 'sacr-ed' by human action....Holiness belongs to the divine, to God alone."[54]

The test, as mentioned earlier, of whether the sacred symbols, rituals, convictions, moral practices, and pattern of common life in the community are leading to the Holy ("healthy-sacred") is whether reverence, gratefulness, joy, silence, creativity, courage, justice, forgiveness, compassion, and praise and penitence in the presence of the Holy One are actually being lived in the community.

There is profound hubris in claims that our sacred system comprehends the Holy One precisely and exclusively. And this hubris has given rise to much xenophobia, triumphalism, and ultimately murder. Sheer identification of divine mystery with human agency must always lead to exclusivism and exclusivism to fanaticism,

In discussing an "epistemology of Revelation" in *Principles of*

Christian Theology, John Macquarrie, following Heidegger, distinguishes calculative and primordial thinking. Calculative thinking is concerned for "handling, using, manipulating this object..."; primordial thinking has "a meditative character...,[it] waits and listens...."[55] The notion of revelation as a deposit of faith (really a deposit of beliefs), arises from the dominance of calculative over primordial thinking. This is not chiefly a plot to manipulate God for corrupt purposes, although it has often had that effect. It arises rather from the ontic limitations, the sheer finitude, of the created order. Things are either true or false for us; God's name is really either Allah or Yahweh or Brahma. This is the notion of truth in the image of property: if it's mine, it's not yours.

But, is it possible to give sufficient devotion to the symbols, rituals, convictions, moral practices, and patterns of common life of my religious community while acknowledging their origin in human searching for the divine? In Rahner's words, is it possible to acknowledge and to live out the difference between "categorical revelation" and "transcendental revelation"?[56] It must be. When women and men of good faith see the destructive effects of conflating the sacred and the holy, they will ultimately accept the historical, rather than ontological, status of the sacred. The efficacy of these sacred symbols, rituals, convictions, moral practices, and patterns of common life will be confirmed by the witness of lives of greater holiness, and fear of relativism will ebb.

The difficulty of the question is further clarified by considering again the work of the distinguished Jewish theologian, David Novak. His book, *Jewish-Christian Dialogue: A Jewish Justification*, is a model of openness, clarity, and sensitivity. He is one of the principle authors of the deeply reconciling statement "Dabru Emet: A Jewish Statement On Christians and Christianity," published in September 2000. Yet even Novak can write that syncretism undermining the integrity of a religious community's life lies in "each side...overcom[ing] the exclusivity of its truth claims." This "destroy[s] the very basis of the truth claims of both Judaism and Christianity."[57] In contrast, the thesis here is that disavowing that my community's truth claims are exclusively the truth does not undermine the community; it liberates it. The claims are true but not exclusively so.

Speaking of "relativism," Novak says it is the community laying aside "the proper assertion…to be the most adequate fulfillment of the ultimate requirement of human nature in this world, which is to be related to God."[58] This is a remarkable statement for one so deeply and genuinely engaged in interreligious work—though perhaps it is not so surprising. When such work is understood to culminate in dialogue but not go beyond to deeper works of spiritual companionship, the contradiction between asserting, on the one hand, a claim of "most adequate fulfillment" of relatedness to God, and on the other, God's radical self-communication to all that has been brought into existence by superabundant divine love, is perhaps inevitable.

Relativism, and the syncretism which sometimes accompanies it, does not lie in setting aside exclusive claims to truth. It lies in compromising the clarity and sincerity with which the sacred symbols, rituals, convictions, moral practices, and patterns of common life are embodied in the spiritual practice of the members of the religious community. It is a foolish mixing of elements of sacred systems or cynical manipulation of these sacred elements or allowing their corruption through want of continuous reformation that may lead to syncretism and relativism. It is when the sacred does not point to the Holy and the religion lacks vitality, that syncretism and relativism abound. Novak claims that avowing exclusive truth claims, or claims of greater adequacy, "is nothing less than conceding the fundamentally human constitution of the relationship with God…a form of idolatry."[59] But it is in fact idolatry to deny the "human constitution" of the elements of the sacred system, especially the "sacred convictions," the truth claims. As Panikkar writes: "The actual pole for all our truth utterances is not a divine or perfect intellect but human consciousness, individual or collective, situated in space, time, matter, culture and so forth. We have to take our own contingency very seriously, and our grandeur lies precisely in the awareness of our limitations."[60]

I said that renouncing exclusive truth claims is liberating. It liberates the leaders and other members of a religious community from triumphalism. And it obliges those within the community—in some sense all members of the community—who "handle" one or another of the sacred elements (religious educators, for example) to do so with creativity and sincerity.

This is so the "truth" of a community's symbols, rituals, convictions, moral practices, and patterns of common life is verified in the faithfulness of lives formed in that community. Whereas a notion of my religion's truthfulness based on an *a priori* "most true," "only true," or "most adequate" status of its revelation is not only an evasion but also a corruption. It is with an eye on both the brutal history of exclusive religious truth claims and on the anemic religious education practice which flows from *a priori* assumptions of religious superiority, that Gabriel Moran writes: "To make revelation into an object of believing has been a disaster."[61]

Religious traditions are not true or false; they are either signatory or they fail to signal, to awaken, to make aware, to disclose, or to point. Jaroslav Pelikan understands this fully. Speaking of tradition as "icon," Pelikan underlines both the contingent character of truth claims and the defining role of devotion to my religious community's sacred elements as my way of living well: "Tradition qualifies as an icon...when it does not present itself as co-extensive with the truth it teaches, but does present itself as the way that we who are its heirs must follow if we are to go beyond it; through it, but beyond it."[62]

Education Practice

Later, in chapter five ("Praying Together"), I will deal with what I believe is the most important religious education element in deepening spiritual encounter and forging spiritual companionship between members of different religious communities. This is contemplation education. Now I place the thesis of this book in a broader context of religious education practice.

The functions of religious education are dialectically related to each other. That is, the functions are in some tension with one another but can co-exist and enrich each other. The principal dialectical function of religious education is to both nurture the faithfulness of the members of the religious community through its sacred symbols, rituals, convictions, moral practices and patterns of common life, and also to promote a climate within the community conducive to deep interreligious encounter. This dialectical pairing is what Moran means by the distinction between "teaching to be religious" and "teaching a religion."

Dialectical pairings are common in mainstream or progressive (or liberal) Christian religious education, though not so in the more sectarian traditions including even many moderate evangelical communities. Several generations of scholars of religious education in the United States came to know this progressive tradition (literally, that religious education within the community is always about a set of dialectically related functions) by being introduced to the work of the seminal twentieth-century theorist, George Albert Coe. Coe's way of describing the dual (and dialectically related) functions of religious education was to ask, as he did in his masterful 1917 work, *A Social Theory of Religious Education*, whether the purpose of religious education is to "pass on a religion or to change the world."[63] For Coe the answer was both.

More recently, Thomas Groome has spoken of the dual—and dialectical—function as bringing the inherited story of the religious community into critical correlation with the present vision of that community and reinterpreting both, thereby living the story and the vision anew. This view is indebted to the conciliar reforms envisioned by Pope John XXIII and Pope Paul VI. Groome's formula has meaning only if one believes, as the Council taught, that there is something revelatory in the "signs of the times."[64]

The theological influence working in Coe's thought was liberal Christianity, deriving especially from Schleiermacher and Ritschl and emphasizing historical consciousness and moral passion. Groome is deeply influenced by the biblical and theological renaissance culminating at the Second Vatican Council. As classically expressed by such theologians as David Tracy, to whose method of critical correlation Groome is indebted, this view replaces a static scholasticism with rich biblical narrative, historical consciousness, and an anthropocentric focus on the Christian believer as, in Rahner's term, "hearer of the word."[65]

Though both Coe and Groome's formulations of the proper scope of religious education practice provide openness to interreligious work, neither writes with this explicit intention. The focus in each case is on renewing the vitality of Christian life, though later in life Coe's purposes became more profoundly secular. Gabriel Moran, on the other hand, writes with a radical ecumenical openness, and his attention to interreligious reverence is explicit, as we shall see. And Mary Boys and Sara Lee call their practice "educating for religious particularity and pluralism."[66]

Boys first spoke of "tradition" and "transformation," and the transformative power of reinterpreting traditions so that the religious community moves beyond triumphalism in its perception of its relationship with the "others." The transformation Boys envisions is at once a vital purification of the internal life of the religious community and one which brings about a far greater openness to other spiritual paths and those on them. More recently, she has written of "religious communities that are at once clear and ambiguous, rooted and adaptive."[67]

We see similar impulses linking firmness of commitment in religious communities to openness and regard for others and their religious communities in Jewish thinkers such as Rabbis David Hartman, Leon Klenicki, and Eric Yoffie, as well as Irving Greenberg, to whom reference was made in chapter one. Hartman, for example, asks: "Can I happily see Christians in their passionate love for what mediates the spiritual life for them? Can I celebrate their joy and yet not feel that my joy of mitzvah is weakened?"[68] Klenicki proposes that alongside ecclesiastical triumphalism there may be a "triumphalism of memory," (which he also sometimes refers to as a "triumphalism of pain"), that blocks Jews advancing to a stage of deeper spiritual encounter:

> I feel the need to understand the other as a person of God. Can this be done? Can I really be a religious person putting aside a fellow community that is rooted in my own allegiance to God? Can I disregard two thousand years of history, avoiding the representatives of that covenantal relationship? Can I look into the first century and neglect to see God's call to Jesus and the early Christians? Can the pain of history alienate me as it did Christians for centuries? Can I learn to think about Christianity through an encounter with Christians?[69]

Eric Yoffie's perspective is equally pointed and helpful, though it is limited by the assumptions of a "stage three" view of the fullness of relations, one that ends in satisfying and useful theological dialogue. Still, there is no doubting the strength of Yoffe's critique or that he is advocating adoption in Jewish education of a dual, if not fully dialectical, function.

> ...in our community we have failed utterly in conveying to our young people the revolutionary changes that have taken place in the Church since the Second Vatican Council. Too often we teach nothing at all about other religious traditions to our children and what we do teach about Catholicism is likely to focus on the Inquisition and the Crusades. This is a moral failure of the first order and we have a profound responsibility to provide an immediate remedy.[70]

Yoffie calls for "positive religious education": "This means that Catholics need to educate Catholics about Jews and Jews need to educate Jews about Catholics....we should review your books and you should review ours. And we should not hesitate to prod, push and make demands on ourselves and on each other."[71]

Religious and theological educators mentioned thus far do not understand the interreligious function of religious education in the same ways. Their differences are more than nuances. It is arguable, for example, whether any of them except Moran would subscribe to the thesis of this book, though Mary Boys' view comes closest to the other religious thinkers both Christian and Jewish, as I suggested in chapter one. Remember that the 1993 to 1995 Colloquium of Jewish and Catholic educators which she and Sara Lee convened was called the Educating for Religious Particularity and Pluralism Project.

But among Christian scholars who take account of the dual (and dialectically related) functions of religious education, none are more open to deepened spiritual encounter in terms broadly similar to those discussed here than Gabriel Moran. Alongside his bracing treatment of revelation, about which more in chapter three, there are three other features of Moran's scholarship about practice of religious education that mark him as the definitive scholar in the field promoting real spiritual companionship. First, Moran never conflates education and schooling. One can see how easily this occurs in the quote cited before, from Rabbi Yoffie, who jumps immediately from the "need to educate Catholics about Jews and Jews...about Catholics," to the recommendation that we "should review your books and you should review ours." Moran would never make the simple jump from "education" to "books." For him, education occurs within four "social forms," not one. These are family, school, job, and leisure. At the very least, this provides a much broader range of human experience and practice out of which a greater depth of recognition of one another and our common spiritual yearnings can emerge. The approach that de-absolutizes schooling also relativizes what in most Jewish-Christian dialogues is currently absolute, namely theological discourse.

In this same vein, Rabbi Heschel writes:

> We suffer from the fact that our understanding of religion today has been reduced to ritual, doctrine, institution, symbol, theology detached from the *pre-theological* (Rabbi Heschel's emphasis) situation, the pre-symbolic depth of existence....we must lay bare what is involved in religious existence; we must recover the situations which both precede and correspond to the theological formulations; we must recall the questions [arising from everyday life in family, work, play as well as school] which religious doctrines try to answer, the antecedents of religious commitment, the presuppositions of faith.[72]

The second feature is Moran's view of the evolution of religious education through three stages across the span of healthy human (and communal) development. Here it becomes clear that Moran's is a view that doesn't simply "account" for the others: coming to see ourselves as spiritual companions of all other women and men who are on the same journey is intrinsic to Moran's view. In his treatment of the stages, Moran further stipulates the functions of religious education in a healthy religious community, going beyond the dual functions to which reference has been made to a fuller threefold practice. Moran envisions early childhood religious formation as "simply religious" education, as simply (not so simply!) clearing negatives from the child's path of human development, resisting violence of any kind directed at the child and supporting the child's imagination and openness to awe. This is a practice that defends what Maria Montessori called the child's natural contemplative capacity. It is at a second stage, not this first stage but a second one of "acquiring a religion," that the visions and narratives, the rituals and the convictions of the child's religious community are the appropriate content of religious education. The distinction of functions in the context of human development is crucial: a too early confessional initiation of the wrong kind may produce sectarian fixity, "acquiring a religion" of absolute and exclusive claims.

For Moran the culmination of faithfulness lived out in religious communities, his third stage, is becoming "religiously Christian (Jewish, Muslim) and so forth." He writes: "Religious education at this stage is not the building of one's case to score against our adversaries. It is a journey of compassion for every human being who, no matter what his or her beliefs, is recognized, accepted and loved as a fellow traveler on this earth."[73]

Over many years of profound reflection on lives and practices in religious communities, Moran has never lost sight of the idea that the purpose of such living is not the triumph of religion but the journey toward holiness. He calls the final (sixth) "moment," occurring during this third stage of "religious education development," the moment of "detachment and centering" and writes of it: "As imagination expands and the mind is quieted, we come to see similarities among all things. Simultaneously we become detached from superficial perceptions of the self and from the apotheosis of any object. The journey [is] to the One beyond all names."[74]

The difficulties, to say it again, of leaders and other members of religious communities actually practicing religious education in this fashion are real. Fayette Veverke's reflection on these difficulties is especially helpful not only because her treatment is so clear and informed by social scientific insight about communities but also because Veverke is so committed to enhancing interreligious—especially Jewish-Christian—relations.

Noting as I did earlier that a call to deepen and expand relations across "boundaries" is imperiled by centrifugal forces that tend to dissolve religious communities, Veverke writes: "It is not unreasonable for Jews and Christians to anticipate that interreligious dialogue may intensify and accelerate the destabilizing, decentering forces that persistently undermine communal traditions, authorities and values."[75]

Veverke notes quite correctly that for dialogue to continue and deepen, we "must be prepared to argue clearly and persuasively that educating for authentic particularity and responsible pluralism are intrinsically related, not mutually exclusive...[and] that identity is ultimately sustained not by guarding boundaries but by maintaining a vital communal life."[76]

Veverke has named precisely the point I wish to affirm in this book. Religious particularity of its own often leads to triumphalism and the consequent corruption of the community. Much exclusivism in the history of religions is an evasion of the obligation to build vital communities. We will not have religious communities whose members, while particular in their loyalties and practices, are at the same time profoundly committed to pluralism until the relationship (and differentiation) between religion and spirituality is more broadly appreciated and until the dual functions of education in religious communities are more broadly and effectively practiced. This will not happen until the notion of truth claims in the image of private property dissolves.

Crossing a border beyond even profound dialogue and passionate common engagement in moral practice to a "place" of spiritual companionship will not occur until the ways in which exclusivism impoverishes and corrupts the religious community are fully acknowledged. But after the border is crossed, we may experience the profundity of Moran's remark that "to accept life in a community is implicitly an affirmation of life itself. It is a recognition that this people that I call my people is an embodiment of the universal human community."[77] Growing affirmation of our own and other's religious communities is a work of religious education.

Appreciating Christianity

In my 1997 book, *The Enduring Covenant: The Education of Christians and the End of Antisemitism*,[78] there is a chapter entitled "The Genius of Judaism." The book, as the subtitle says, is intended to educate Christians in the sorry history of the "teaching of contempt," the need for interreligious reverence and the necessary changes in Christian theological interpretation and religious educational practice for ending antisemitism influenced by anti-Jewish Christian perspectives. The chapter on Judaism is intended to replace prejudicial perspectives based on inaccuracy and stereotype with a richer more appreciative understanding of some of the defining realities of Judaism in its biblical, theological, moral, and communal expressions. The chapter treats nine features of Judaism: a Jewish view of the divine-human relationship, human relations, human knowing, suffering, moral life, spiritual life, law, chosenness, and land. Following Robert Coles' injunction that the most effective means of growing morally and spiritually is to "attend to the saints in our midst," the chapter concludes with a sketch of a paradigmatic Jewish figure, not surprisingly, Rabbi Abraham Joshua Heschel.

In a similar vein, chapter four of this book, "How Reverence Emerges," will contain a sympathetic portrait of selected, but defining, features of Christianity. This is intended for both Jewish and Christian readers, but just as the chapter on Judaism in my earlier book was intended primarily for a Christian readership, "How Reverence Emerges" is first of all directed at Jewish and other non-Christian readers. Its purpose, however, is not apologetic but, as noted in chapter one, the enrichment that follows when the religious convictions of others are seen to illumine common religious experiences. To cite Krister Stendahl again, how can we love one another if we do not know some profound things about one another: what makes us happy, what makes us sad? Or Rabbi Heschel, who says: "My first task in every encounter is to comprehend the personhood of the human being I face, to sense the kinship of being, solidarity of being."[79]

What Heschel speaks of with reference to encounter between human beings seems equally applicable to religious communities. For a stage of spiritual companionship to be approached, Jews must know more about what Christians believe and the religious experiences expressed in these beliefs.

But what then of Christianity to highlight and examine? Which of the myriad elements of so complex a reality hold the greatest promise of making faithfulness in the Christian key transparent? And which elements, if any, may provide Jewish spiritual companions with clues from Christianity that may be useful on their own way of faithfulness?

Before answering, we need to entertain at greater length the caution expressed by Michael Kogan, mentioned briefly in chapter one. In a remarkably sensitive essay on Jewish-Christian relations, Kogan asks: "If God is the author of the Christian faith as God is of ours, then we must ask this question: would God act in such a way as to bring the nations to know God by means of fraudulent claims?" Kogan then treats defining Christian doctrinal convictions including the "incarnation of God in Jesus" and "the resurrection of Jesus from the dead" with great openness and theological clarity. But he adds immediately: "While we can and should deepen our self-understanding through dialogue with our sister faith, adoption of any part of the kerygma of Christianity would be for us as inauthentic as it is unnecessary."[80] This would truly be a corrupting syncretism and relativism. It would be the furthest thing from Krister Stendahl's idea, mentioned in chapter one, of "holy envy": "when we recognize something in the other tradition that is beautiful but is not ours, nor should we grab it or claim it....Holy envy rejoices in the beauty of the other."[81]

But when we see and understand the convictions of the other as illuminating common religious experiences, then we recognize the other as a companion, and in Moran's phrase, we embark on "a journey of compassion, a fellow traveler on this earth." Instead of seeming bizarre and anomalous, the symbols, rituals, convictions, moral practices, and patterns of common life within the religious community of the other are seen and appreciated as instruments nurturing in them and their community qualities of reverence, gratefulness, joy, silence, creativity, courage, justice, forgiveness, compassion, and praise and penitence in front of the Holy One. Then, across religious communities, those of us with conscious spiritual yearnings are less alone in a so-called culture of disbelief.

The choice in my earlier book of aspects of Judaism to reinterpret and celebrate, free of stereotype, was in some ways easier and less arbitrary than here. Some features were chosen because of the primal contribution of Jewish spiritual genius to the other great Abrahamic religions, as well as to culture in general, is disclosed by reinterpreting these features more accurately and appreciatively. The discussion of the divine-human relationship is one such element. A second kind of issue was chosen strictly to dissipate an historic distortion. Topics such as "law" and "chosenness" are examples.

Here I have chosen to approach the usefulness of Christian belief to an other by asking the reader to:

1. listen to a contemporary liberal Christian theological voice on the Church, the doctrine of Christ and the moral life;
2. listen to a contemporary liberal Christian theological voice distinguish the streams within Catholicism of "ecclesiastical-institutional Catholicism" and the stream of "spiritual-intellectual-theological Catholicism";
3. listen to a portrait of a paradigmatic figure in a Christian way of faithfulness, the figure of Thomas Merton.

The format takes us through theological dialogue to a deeper encounter. The first two invite theological reflection, clarity and appreciation. But considering the great spiritual master, Thomas Merton, is an exercise in what Heschel called depth theology for it goes to the essence of the way of faithfulness as lived in revealing the spiritual genius of a worthy companion.

Liberal Theological Perspectives on Church, Christ, and Moral Life

A good deal of the most productive "official" contact between Jews and Christians, especially Catholics, effectively brings together deeply conservative Church leaders and Jewish leaders who are indifferent to theological currents. By "productive," I mean contacts that lead to consultations resulting in various official documents that eschew historical Christian positions that are anti-Jewish; joint papers that articulate broad similarities or affinities between Judaism and Christianity or collaborations that lead to educational programs (often really only "instructional" programs) in which Jews and Christians of various ages study one another's traditions or, finally, more action-oriented initiatives in the realm of social policy and practice. (In this catalogue I am not including meetings between learned Jewish and Christian religious thinkers since these, by definition, are concerned with one another's genuine sense of self-identity).

One may question the full extent of the "productivity" of the engagements noted above. Productive from what ideological perspective, or how productive and toward what ideological ends? When, for example, one reads of satisfaction on the part of some Jewish leaders with the 1998 Vatican document, *We Remember: A Reflection on the Shoah*, or—the companion piece—a steady stream of news reports that convey that only "Jewish leaders" were disappointed with exculpatory elements in that document, the limits of productivity when official relations often join only conservative church officials and theologically indifferent or naïve Jewish leaders begins to dawn.

This is not to dismiss the extraordinary work which continues to be accomplished by just such leadership and their constituencies, as I have already noted. There are, however, at least three reasons why a theological conversation between Jews and Christians needs to be deepened and to include more fully the liberal Christian theological voice. First, for Jewish leaders to be indifferent to or ignorant of the theological assumptions of conservative church leaders with whom they work may lead to pyrrhic victories in improving relations over the long run.

Second, for Jews who seek a more broadly intelligible theological explanation for their own experience and who believe this goal is in part served by interreligious theological discourse, it is more "productive" to engage a range of Christian theological positions. And, I think, the contemporary liberal Christian theological consensus on a range of issues, including those in chapter four, is more satisfying than the contemporary conservative, let alone ultra-conservative, positions. Third, like Christians moving to a relationship of spiritual companionship with Jews, Jews of like loyalties and aspirations are required to listen (and to speak) to this broader range of theological opinion.

In addition, I simply hope a time will come when more Jews, engaged in these relations, come to appreciate the richness of much of the contemporary liberal Christian theological consensus on the theology of the Church, the doctrine of Christ, and on moral life. To this is added the hope that more Jewish persons will come to appreciate the affinity of the interpretations within this consensus to a rich stream of Jewish thought and practice.

But, there are two problems with identifying theological discourse between Jews and Christians as "liberal," no matter how carefully one seeks to distinguish theological liberalism from its other expressions. The first is that "mainstream" or "liberal" Protestant churches in the United Sates are perceived as predominantly pro-Palestinian and anti-Zionist. There are many reasons for this, and it is not simply a matter of perception but of fact. Mainstream Protestant Christian leaders in this country, focused with great compassion on the plight of Palestinians and rightly critical of certain actions of the Likud party in Israel, have simply not dealt with as much evenhandedness as one would like with the parallel need of Israelis for security against terrorism. Part of this reality is simply empathy for the overtly poor and marginal. And part of it can be ascribed to a fundamental difference in affinity, at a fairly deep social and religious level, between American Jews and liberal Protestant Christians on the one hand, and American Catholics and Jews on the other. At this writing, the leadership of the worldwide Anglican Communion, as well as that of the World Council of Churches, is debating devestment in Israel as a means of advancing the Middle East peace process.

The second problem is misunderstanding theological liberalism, misunderstanding the theological method called "liberal." It is the idea that theological liberalism is virtually identical to relativism. For example, the English Jewish scholar Norman Solomon writes of liberal Jewish and Christian theologians having little difficulty reaching "accommodations" because both share "relativist" positions: "denying that any theology is ultimately superior to any other."[82] Solomon is wrong on two counts. First, as noted already, relativism need not result from shedding views about the superiority of our views over others. Second, religions and their theological explanations are not superior and inferior. Theologies are functional or dysfunctional. They either promote spiritual life, by clarifying the authentic way of a religious community, or they do not. Relativism arises when the spiritual vitality of a religious tradition is undermined, not when members of the community acknowledge humbly that the Holy One is present to many peoples on many paths of spiritual life, in many religious communities.

As noted in chapter one, theological liberalism takes account of historical development and ordinary patterns of common human experience in construing the meaning of the religious community's symbols, rituals, convictions, moral practices, and common patterns.

> The modern or liberal impulse is the source for grounding religious loyalties in continuing human experience, subjecting inherited traditions of interpretation of religious beliefs to historical analysis, exploring the context of sacred texts and rejecting the imposition of absolute interpretations by authoritarian and triumphalist ecclesiastical powers in favor of freedom of inquiry and relativity (in the sense of openness to change and growth).[83]

On the Church, a consensus exists among liberal Catholics, mainline Protestants, and some moderate evangelical Christians. The consensus holds that the fundamental character of the Church is communal, not hierarchic. This holds true even where Christians embrace a hierarchic role within the church community. Liberal Christians will appeal back over the centuries during which an autocratic hierarchy evolved to the early Church in which bishops were often chosen from within and by the community, and their authority was understood as deriving from charism (gift of the Holy Spirit) and not chiefly from their juridical designation as bishops. Cyprian, the fifth-century North African bishop, will be quoted approvingly by theological liberals in this regard: "I have made it a rule ever since the beginning of my episcopate to make no decision merely on the strength of my own personal opinion without consulting you (the priests and the deacons) and without the approbation of the people."[84]

And, as Garry Wills has pointed out, Saint Augustine's view of his ministry as bishop, the depth of his sense of responsibility to the community which he served, stands in marked contrast to an autocratic episcopacy. Augustine writes: "For you I am a bishop; with you I am a Christian."[85]

In sketching this essentially communal model of the Church, I hope Jewish as well as Christian readers will appreciate the profound implications of the appeal back over the centuries in which Constantinian structures of power and authority evolved. It is not beside the point that a communal model bears affinity to a defining pattern in Jewish theology, dating back to the prophet Isaiah's strictures against the whole Jewish community, but most especially the kingly and priestly leaders, if even a single orphan or widow is denied justice and compassion.[86]

The liberal Christian theological consensus on the doctrine of Christ (christology) has moved away from a predominant emphasis on a metaphysical christology, with Christ embedded in dogmatic language that makes universal claims for this king's preeminent place in a cosmic drama of fall and redemption. A more contemporary and liberal emphasis might be called "existential." In this framework, dogmatic claims are not so important as emotional engagement, through preaching and eucharistic practice, with the human person, Jesus Christ, who is himself, through grace, aligned so deeply with the transcendent Holy One. God, as Plotinus said, is the "Center of centers," and Jesus Christ is understood as uniquely centered in the Divine Center.

The Christian is centered in Jesus Christ through prayer and emulation. This is sometimes called "action christology." Its purpose is not to shore up truth claims but to evoke purity of heart, the near universal religious image for the authentic self.[87] In an existential emphasis, the cross of Christ is one of human history's sublime expressions of human persons coming to terms, in hope and courage, with suffering and pain. The death and resurrection of Jesus Christ are real and happen to Jesus. They are, as well, metaphor (but as the Catholic theologian, David Power writes, not "mere metaphor")[88] for the continuous work of dying and rising of the follower of Christ: dying to fear and selfishness, despair, and self-absorption and rising reverent, grateful, joyous, silent, creative, courageous, just, forgiving, compassionate and praising, and penitent before God.

Again, one does not wish for any Jew to adopt any feature of the Christian kerygma. But it is noteworthy that when the doctrine of Christ is stripped of the kind of dogmatic language which Power refers to as "naïve realism,"[89] its essential meaning—about the intimacy of the relationship between the divine and the human—is easily linked to covenantal Jewish theology. The link is certainly obscured by christological language which simply conflates God and Jesus, so that Jews and Muslims detect a threat to monotheism rather than a teaching which points to this intimacy of relationship as proposed in the Book of Genesis.

A liberal Christian theological consensus on the moral life reveals yet another affinity, or correspondence, with a rich vein of Judaism. Though Pope John Paul II sought, in his 1998 encyclical, *Splendor Veritas*, ("The Splendor of Truth"), to reassert a "classicist" foundation for moral thinking, the liberal Christian theological consensus on moral life, setting aside classicism, embraces historical consciousness. Richard B. Mc Brien explains the distinction and the shift:

> Classicism conceives the moral life of a Christian as that which conforms to certain preexisting norms; divine law, natural law, ecclesiastical law....It is deductive rather than inductive and it deals with moral issues in the abstract, i.e., according to universal norms rather than in the light of particular or even peculiar circumstances and situations....Historical consciousness, on the other hand, conceives the moral life of the Christian as one of personal responsibility within changing historical conditions. Indeed, the norms themselves reflect the historical situation in which they were first formulated and subsequently interpreted. The emphasis, then, is on the "subject" as historical and social....It deals more with moral issues in the concrete and in terms of the particulars of the historical moment.[90]

Historical consciousness is the basis for the perspective on moral thinking called "proportionalism." The Catholic moral theologian, Timothy O'Connell, explains "two truths" on which proportionalism rests: "The first truth is that human persons are finite...all our human choices involve the resolution of conflicts....What makes a particular behavior morally right is the fact that it is as helpful as possible, given the alternatives....The second truth [is] that of temporality, the reality of time, of change....Although past experience teaches us much...the possibility of something truly, powerfully, new remains one of the challenges we face."

Taking account of these truths, the formal proportionalist position then is this: "the best one can do is to be faithful to the complex and changing circumstances of our lives, doing as much good as possible and as little harm as necessary."[91] The position is akin to the Jewish view captured in the Hebrew phrase *P'kuach Nefesh* (or *P'kuach Neshema*), "to save a life," according to which any legal obligation, except to abstain from murder, rape, and incest, may be set aside to save a life. More broadly, here is a moral realism which warns us off moral absolutism whose satisfying certainties often lead to fanaticism and inhumanity.

And this is not the only affinity between a rich vein of Jewish moral thinking and the contemporary liberal Christian theological consensus on moral life. The other great transformation in Christian moral life in our time is recovering the primacy of the common good over individual desire. The idea is enshrined in Christian scripture as well as medieval communitarian ethics. It reappears in various Christian liberation theologies today in the preference shown for practice of justice and peace over merely formal observance or inert assent to doctrine, in the preference, as liberation theologians so often put it, for *orthopraxis* over *orthodoxis* (for "right practice" over "right belief"). This development in Christianity is a retrieval of Jewish communitarianism. And it is for this reason, as noted earlier, that the distinguished Catholic theologian David Tracy has characterized the contemporary liberation theologies as a re-Judaizing of Christianity.[92]

Catholic Church, Catholic Spirit

Another element of chapter four will distinguish "ecclesial-institutional Catholicism" and "spiritual-intellectual Catholicism." Here there can be no question of a simple dichotomy, let alone a Manichaean one, where "Catholic Church" is the realm of bureaucratic darkness and "Catholic spirit" the realm of spiritual light.

The Catholic Church, even today after over two decades of a restorationist papacy overseen by a pope of such compelling strengths, bears some remarkable resemblances to the Constantinian Catholic Church of earlier times. This is the Church of absolutist teaching style and autocratic exercise of authority. In its early centuries, it evolved as a response to the Church's increasingly prominent role as a source of order in a crumbling Roman Empire.

Nurtured in this same Catholic Church but existing in uneasy relationship to triumphalism, there is the Catholic spirit. It is a spirituality that is deeply humanistic, emphasizing the goodness of all that emanates from divine love. It is a sacramental spirit insisting that all of human life and experience carries potential for evoking the presence of the Holy One. Where the Catholic Church, the "official" church, acts in a contrary way, most famously in its cramped view of sexuality, for example, it is at profound odds with the Catholic spirit itself. But again, it will be important in the fuller discussion of this feature of a contemporary liberal Catholic theological consensus to strike a balance and avoid false dichotomy. For even in the midst of restoration, there are many ideological crosscurrents in the Catholic Church. And although more than enough Catholic fundamentalists are on the scene, much conflict over the direction of the Catholic Church, and its faithfulness to the Catholic spirit, is waged between genuine liberals and genuine conservatives. Very real questions of balance between tradition and modernity, order and change, authority and freedom are joined and must be examined thoughtfully. The intent of this analysis will not be so much to criticize a triumphal ecclesiastical party as to reveal to the reader the rich, humanistic core of Catholic spirituality.

Thomas Merton, Exemplar

Finally, the effort to evoke that spirituality and generate appreciation for it, rests on its embodiment in the great spiritual teacher Thomas Merton (1915-1968).

Thomas Merton lived a searching if essentially dissolute life until his conversion in 1938 and entrance into a Trappist monastery in 1941. In the ensuing twenty-seven years as a monk, he played a pivotal role in renewing practice of contemplative prayer, promoting appreciation for the spiritual richness of many religious traditions, encouraging generations to link spiritual yearning with action for justice and peace, especially with regard to the civil rights and anti-war movements of mid-century. Merton nurtured leaders of liberation theology in Latin America and was, as the saying goes, "ahead of the curve" in promoting reconciliation between Jews and Christians

Merton was fearless in his work of striving to live well, to frame a masterpiece of reverence, gratefulness, joy, silence, creativity, courage, justice, forgiveness, compassion and praise, and penitence before the Holy One. He is supremely estimable for the integrity of his effort, the sheer honesty of his pursuit of a genuine self, and avoidance of pseudo-identity or what he called the "false self," or alternately, "exterior I," in contrast to "true self" or "interior I." Added to this is the wit and learning, the hilarity and curiosity that he brought to this work, and the manner in which a lifelong engagement with solitude helped him achieve heights of human compassion. All this makes him truly a "man for all seasons" and a witness for many people on many disparate paths of spirituality in many different religious communities.

Notes

1. S. Heschel, op cit., p. 29.
2. For an incisive treatment of the falsehood surrounding Pius XII's cause for canonization, see Garry Wills, *Papal Sins: Structures of Deceit* (New York: Doubleday, 2000), pp 61–69.
3. Tracy, op. cit., pp 27–31.
4. Stephen Carter, *The Culture of Disbelief: How American Law and Politics Trivialize Religious Devotion* (New York: Basic Books, 1993).
5. S. Heschel, op. cit., p. 295.
6. "Both communication and separation are necessary. We must preserve our individuality as well as foster care for one another, reverence, understanding, cooperation." Ibid. p. 241.

7. "In the Pope's Words: The Echo of the Heart Rending Laments." *New York Times*, March 16, 2000.

8. "Statement on the Catechism of the Catholic Church," *Professional Approaches for Christian Educators,* PACE volume 24, September, 1994, p 43. Signed by the Catholic members of the Christian Scholars Group on Judaism and the Jewish People.

9. Wills, op. cit., p. 65. The document released by the Vatican Commission for Religious Relations with the Jews is entitled "We Remember: A Reflection on the Shoah." Vatican Congregation for Religious Relations with the Jews, March 16, 1998.

10. See David I. Kertzer, *The Kidnapping of Edgardo Montaro* (New York: Alfred A. Knopf, 1997).

11. From Ignatius of Antioch, cited by Wills, op. cit., p. 141.

12. Ibid., p. 5. Wills employs the word "man" because he is speaking principally of honest parish priests who can hardly bare to promulgate some of what comes from episcopal and Vatican sources.

13. The distinction is that between the exaltation of assent to propositions of belief (*orthodoxis*) over genuinely living a life in imitation of Jesus, a prayerful life in which one acts for justice and for peace (*orthopraxis*).

14. Here is Msgr. Carolos Liberati, realtor, promoter, of the cause for canonization of Pope Pius IX, "The realtor of the cause of Pope Pius IX for canonization commenting on the kidnapping of Edgardo Montaro: 'if we focus on this minor fact we cannot understand this great pope...,' he said, '...The Church has tried everything to improve relations with the Jews. But they don't forgive us the slightest thing.'" in "Italian Jews Denounce Decision to Canonize Pius IX," *New York Times*, June 28, 2000.

15. In Flannery, op.cit., p. 573.

16. *Catechism of the Catholic Church*, p. 320 #1257, Liberia Editrice Vaticano.

17. S. Heschel, op. cit., p. 239f.

18. James Carroll, "The Silence," *New Yorker*, April 17, 1997, p. 67.

19. Rani Rashkover, "Jewish Responses to Jewish-Christian Dialogue: A Look Ahead to the Twenty-first Century," *Cross Currents* Spring/Summer 2000, p. 213. I am indebted to Rashkover for this preliminary assessment of Soloveitchick's position.

20   Ibid.

21. Ibid., p. 214.

22. Ibid, quoted by Rashkover from "Confrontations."

23. Jules Issac, *Has Anti-Semitism Roots in Christianity?* (New York: National Conference of Christians and Jews, 1962).

24. Inclusive Christology is the proposition that even the unbaptized who are saved are saved through the saving work (death on the cross) of Jesus Christ.

25. Robley Edward Whitson. *The Coming Convergence of World Religions* (New York: Newman Press, 1971).

26. Carroll, op. cit., see note 18 above.

27. Paul Bauman, "RE: James Carroll, The Church and the Holocaust," *Commonweal*, May 23, 1997.

28. Karl Rahner, *Theological Investigations* (Baltimore: Helicon Press. 1961), p. 148f.

29. Paul Tillich, *Systematic Theology* (Three volumes in one), volume III (Chicago: University of Chicago Press, p.159).

30. Abraham Joshua Heschel, *The Insecurities of Freedom* (New York: Farrar, Straus and Giroux, 1966), p. 119.

31. Mary C. Boys, *Has God...?*, op. cit., p. 248.

32. *God's Mercy Endures Forever: Guidelines on the Presentation of Jews and Judaism in Catholic Preaching*, Washington, DC: National Conference of Catholic Bishops, September 1988, p. 10.

33. From personal conversation with Bishop Stendahl.

34. Carol Ochs, *Song of the Self: Biblical Spirituality and Human Holiness* (Valley Forge, PA: Trinity Press International, 1994), p. 24.

35. Thomas Merton, *Contemplative Prayer* (New York: Image Books Doubleday, 1996), p.24.

36. Ibid., p. 46 (after ellipse p. 56).

37. Everett Fox, *The Five Books of Moses* (New York: Schocken Books,. 1995). Exo 3:14f. God said to Moses "Ehyeh Asher Ehyeh: I will be there howsoever I will be there. And he said: Thus shall you say to the Children of Ehyeh: I will be there sends me to you" p. 273.

38. From the transcript of the interview with Carl Sterns in S. Heschel, op. cit., p. 412.

39. Heschel, op. cit., 1966, p. 9.

40. Talmage, op. cit., p. 86.

41. In J.Kellenberger (ed.), *Inter-religious Models and Criteria* (New York: St. Martin Press, 1993), p. 64.

42. In S. Heschel, op. cit., p. 242.

43. Rashkover, op. cit., p. 218.

44. Heschel, op. cit., p. 117f.

45. S. Heschel, Stern interview, op. cit., p. 405.

46. See note 30 above.

47. For a more balanced, though brief, assessment of what he calls the "collision of two worlds" in Heschel's work, see Jon D. Levenson "The Contradiction of Abraham Joshua Heschel," *Commentary*, July 1998.

48. R. Scott Appleby and Martin Marty (eds), *Fundamentalism and Society* (Chicago: University of Chicago Press, 1990 to 1995, five volumes).

49. Paul Knitter, *No Other Name? A Critical Survey of Christian Attitudes Toward the World Religions* (Maryknoll, NY: Orbis Press, 1988), p. 9.

50. Alan M. Dershowitz, *The Vanishing American Jew: In Search of Jewish Identity for the Next Century* (Boston: Little Brown and Company, 1997), p. 24.

51. Ibid., p. 292.

52. Rahner, *Foundations*, op. cit., p. 116.

53. This at first seemingly radical assertion, appears to remove divine inspiration from the actual artifacts of any religion. It is not so in an existential theological key, however. To say that we make every feature of religion, but from an impulse implanted in us by the Divine, an impulse to return to the Holy One, to be like the Holy One, for ourselves and for others, is to say that all the features of our "sacred systems," our religions, which bring this life into practice and into consciousness are, if indirectly, from the Holy One.

54. Edward Robinson, *Icons of the Sacred* (London: SCM Press, Ltd. 1993), p. 3f and after second ellipsis p. 32f.

55. Macquarrie, *Principles*, p. 82f.

56. Rahner, *Foundations*. In the section "The History of Salvation and Revelation," pp. 138 to 177.

57. David Novak, "Avoiding Charges of Legalism and Antinomianism in Jewish-Christian Dialogue," *Modern Theology*, 16/3 April 2000, p. 276.

58. Ibid., p. 277.

59. Ibid.

60. James B. Wiggins, *In Praise of Religious Diversity* (New York: London, Routledge, 1996), p. 106.

61. Gabriel Moran, *Both Sides: The Story of Revelation* (New York: Paulist Press, 2002), p. 26.

62. Jaroslav Pelikan, *The World's Religions* (San Francisco: Harper Collins, 1991), p. 255.

63. George Albert Coe, *A Social Theory of Religious Education* (New York: Charles Scribner's Sons, 1917), p. 61.

64. Thomas H. Groome, *Christian Religious Education: Sharing Our Story and Vision* (San Francisco: Harper and Row, 1981).

65. Karl Rahner, *Hearers of the Word* (New York: Herder and Herder, 1969).

66. Boys and Lee, op. cit., p. 10.

67. Mary C. Boys, *Jewish-Christian Dialogue: One Woman's Experience* (New York: Paulist Press, 1997), p 86.

68. David Hartman, "Judaism Encounters Christianity Anew," in Eugene Fisher (ed), *Visions of the Other: Jewish and Christian Theologians Assess the Dialogue* (New York: Paulist Press, 1994).

69. Leon Klenicki, "A Hopeful Jewish Reflection on the Year 2000," *ADL*, June 19, 1999, p. 4.

70. Eric H. Yoffie, "Good News, Bad News: Extraordinary Achievement and Current Tension in Catholic-Jewish Relations," The Joseph Klein Lecture on Judaic Affairs, Assumption College, Worcester, MA, March 23, 2000. Printed by the Union of American Hebrew Congregations, p. 9.

71. Ibid. In the gap represented by the ellipsis in this quote, Rabbi Yoffie writes: "This is work we need to do separately, but that we should do in close consultation with each other," a variation on Rabbi Soloveitchick's "veil of conversation."

72. S. Heschel, op. cit., p. 295.

73. Gabriel Moran, *Religious Education Development: Images for the Future* (Minneapolis: Winston Press, 1983), p. 205.

74. Ibid., p. 40.
75. Fayette Veverke, "Bonds, Boundaries, and Border Crossings: Education for Religious, Particularity and Pluralism," Boston College Conference, June 18/19, 2000, p. 6.
76. Ibid., p. 1, and after the ellipse p 6.
77. Moran, *Development*, op.cit., p. 102.
78. See note 30, chapter 1.
79. In S. Heschel, op. cit., p. 238.
80. Michael S. Kogan, "Christian-Jewish Dialogue in the Twenty-first Century: Where Do We Go From Here? A Jewish Reflection," Boston College Conference, June 18/19, 2000, p. 8.
81. Krister Stendahl, "From God's Perspective We Are All Minorities," *Journal of Religious Pluralism*, 2 (1993), p. 3.
82. Norman Solomon, "Themes in Christian-Jewish Relations," in Leon Klenicki (ed), *Toward a Theological Encounter: Jewish Understanding of Christianity* (New York: Paulist Press, 1991), p. 31.
83. O'Hare, *Enduring*, op.cit., p. 50.
84. Letter 14:4 of Cyprian. Quoted in Richard P. McBrien, *Catholicism* (first edition), volume two (Minneapolis: Winston Press), p. 822.
85. Ibid., p. 824, quoted from Sermon 340:1. See also Garry Wills' wonderful treatment of Augustine, the bishop: op. cit., chapters 19 and 20.
86. For example Isaiah 1:21–23.
87. Merton, op.cit., p. 33.
88. David Power, *The Eucharistic Mystery: Revitalizing the Tradition* (New York: Crossroad, 1996), p. 56.
89. Ibid., p. 46.
90. McBrien, op.cit., p. 941f (second edition).
91. Timothy O'Connell, "The Natural Law," *Professional Approaches for Christian Educators*, PACE, volume 21, 1991, pp. 76–79.
92. See note 12 chapter 1.

CHAPTER THREE

Revelation Is No Thing

L ike the last one, this chapter, dealing with what I've already called "the essential theological consideration"[1] in the emergence of a deeper level of reverence between persons in different religious communities, including Jews and Christians, begins with an anecdote. The theological consideration is the question of revelation. And on an adequate account of revelation rests the whole program of interreligious reverence: all of us coming "to encounter one another as siblings, as all God's children."[2]

In the Spring of 2000, a two-day academic symposium brought Catholic, Orthodox, and Protestant pastoral and educational leaders in the work of fostering richer relations between Jews and Christians together with a number of their Jewish counterparts. On the second day, discussion dealt with worship. In the midst of a rich, learned, and frank exchange, a pastoral leader in the Catholic Church expressed the opinion that he didn't think the fact that something in a religious community's liturgy might give offense to someone was sufficient grounds for making a change in that liturgy. The tone suggested its author was proudly resisting "political correctness." The essential point seemed to be protecting or defending (whether needed or not) the celebration in Catholic Eucharist of Jesus Christ as, for Christians, the singular defining symbol of God's self-communication.

Needless to say, for this anecdote to be instructive, the "something" offensive and the "someone" offended need to be stipulated further. I seriously doubt, for example, whether the person who made the remark would have objected when Pope John XXIII took the prayer for the "perfidious Jews" out of the Good Friday liturgy or whether he would have found a Jewish objection in those days to the petition untoward. If the "something" found offensive was, for example, nothing less than the celebration of God's presence in Jesus Christ by Christians at worship, then the someone offended would be in the wrong seminar room, a person so bereft of appreciation for the necessary roots of all parties to interreligious discourse in the richness of their community's way as to be absurdly miscast as a partner in such discourse.

Since there was no such person participating in the symposium, one wonders why such an opinion would be registered. My guess is that despite the level of sophistication and mutual understanding in the room, the author of the defense feared that genuine interreligious discourse, what Leonard Swidler has called "depth dialogue,"[3] compromises a Christian's devotion to Jesus Christ as revelation and path of salvation for Christians. Such fear is groundless. But genuine dialogue (not to mention deeper dimensions of relations than that of dialogue) certainly does challenge claims that Jesus Christ is the only revelation of God and path of salvation. And at what might be called an advanced stage of embrace of religious pluralism, the challenge extends to claims of "most adequate" revelation and path of salvation if these claims are applied to everyone.

Though one might be surprised at such defensiveness at so advanced a symposium (and reminded of H. Richard Niebuhr's observation that "self-defense is the most prevalent source of error in all thinking and perhaps especially in theology"),[4] it is certainly true that this topic of revelation, and its corollary salvation, is of defining importance in interreligious relations.

What was especially suggestive in the remarks that I have recounted was a certain blithefulness with which "giving offense" was dismissed, without irony, as constituting a relevant criterion directing the work of reformation of the religious community's language and ritual practices under the influence of interreligious discourse. I was especially attuned to this dimension (to whether "giving offense" is a relevant factor), thanks to having recently heard a typically insightful remark by

Krister Stendahl.[5] Expressing appreciation for James Carroll's book, *Constantine's Sword*, Stendahl made a point reminiscent of Whitehead's aphorism that it takes an extraordinary mind to undertake the contemplation of the obvious.

Stendahl noted that the catalogues of graduate schools of theology and of seminaries are replete with references to "theology and ethics," but one hardly ever encounters the phrasing or the title "ethics and theology." His point was that in the actual history of religious belief, for example, whether certain theological language has given rise to violence and brutality, makes a moral claim on those whose language has such effects. Years earlier I had encountered a similar idea in Gregory Baum's work *Religion and Alienation*, in his treatment of "critical theology."[6] With regard to the topic at hand, Stendahl was lauding the courage and integrity with which Carroll names the complicitous theological language, especially, for example, language about the cross of Jesus Christ, in the centuries of Christian-inspired anti-Judaism and antisemitism in his uniquely honest study of that history.[7]

The point is that giving an adequate account of revelation makes just such a moral claim on us today. This is so because of the social reality in history to which exclusive claims by many religions have lent themselves and continue to lend themselves, as we know so well. The account is demanded by who God is. And, finally, there can be no deeper spiritual encounter as this work envisions without such an accounting.

I have laid out the theme of working toward a fourth stage (or leap to a new paradigm) of relations between Jews and Christians, and ultimately people in all religious communities and on all spiritual ways. This is a stage of "spiritual companionship" in which "our ways of faithfulness become transparent to one another," a stage, truly a culmination, in which we know each other as "siblings—all God's children."[8]

I have touched briefly thus far on how the nature of religion lends itself to absolute and exclusive claims and on how the "history of contempt" as well as minority status can render Jewish partners understandably reluctant to move further. Note has been taken of how theological language divides us. For we are still waiting, after 450 years, for that *doctra ignoranti*, that "learned ignorance," for which Nicholas of

Cusa longed "when the intellect may raise itself to that simplicity where contradictions coincide."[9] Now we need an account of revelation that undergirds achieving spiritual companionship. And as we begin this account, we do well to keep in mind Rosemary Radford Ruether's two moral principles for the reformation of religious language, and the concrete practice it feeds and which gives rise to the language. The "critical principle," as she calls it, holds that "Whatever denies and diminishes or distorts the full humanity[10] of women [the full humanity of the other], is appraised as not redemptive...presumed not to reflect the divine or an authentic relation to the divine...."[11] And the "prophetic principle" enjoins "a rejection of every elevation of one social group against others as image and agent of God...."[12]

Added to this is a specifically Christian, though by no means exclusively Christian, imperative to "clean up" our theology of revelation on the way to an ever deepening spiritual encounter between people in different religious communities and on different spiritual ways. H. Richard Niebuhr gives voice to this specifically Christian motive, saying: "A revelation that can be used to undergird the claim of Christian faith to empire over the souls of men must be something else than the revelation of the god of that Jesus who in faith emptied himself, made himself of no reputation and refused to claim the kingly crown."[13]

The complexity of the topic of revelation is underscored in this passage from Richard P. McBrien's *Catholicism*:

Is the form of divine self-communication verbal, dramatic, mystical, historical, social, political, natural, cosmic or what? What is communicated or disclosed? Is it facts about God and the "other world"? Is it God's own self? Would we have known that which is revealed even if it were not revealed? If God does indeed reveal, why is it that so many people seem either indifferent to or ignorant of divine revelation? Or is it perhaps very difficult to pick up God's signals of transcendence?[14]

In what follows, revelation will be studied under the following headings 1. revelation and violence; 2. revelation: universal, present, personal and responsive; 3. revelation and "content"; 4. revelation as practical; 5. conclusion. The discussion has but one purpose.

Enhanced reverence for one another across differences of religious community and spiritual path engages us ultimately in the affirmation of friendship itself.

Friendship, Aristotle taught, is only possible between equals. Greek thought lingered on the meaning of friendship, laying out the further conditions that partners to a true friendship 1. enjoy one another's company, 2. have use of each other, loving the good in one another and therefore never flattering, and 3. serve, together, a common good.[15] To acknowledge joyfully that in principle the demonstrably healthy religious community and spiritual way of another is as efficacious as one's own for living in response to divine self-communication is surely the ultimate acknowledgment of equality. In its absence, liking is tainted with a patronizing air and we have no real "use" of one another since we can learn nothing from the other about holiness. Above all, the common good is undermined as the capacity of religious differences to generate social disharmony at least, and violence as often, continues unabated.

Revelation and Violence

Almost a decade before September 11, 2001, Leonard Swidler wrote these prophetic words:

> The future offers two alternatives: death or dialogue....Until the edge of the present era humans lived in the Age of Monologue. That age is now passing. We are now poised at the entrance of the Age of Dialogue....Today nuclear or ecological, or other, catastrophic devastation lies just a little bit further down the path of monologue. It is only by struggling out of the self-centered monologic mindset into dialogue with "the others" as they really are and not as we have projected them in our monologues, that we can avoid such cataclysmic disasters.[16]

The clue that Swidler appreciates not only—and obviously—that dialogue of a certain quality is the alternative to violence but also that he possesses a sense, as he calls it, of "depth dialogue," lies in the telling phrase "the others as they really are." Dialogue with others "as they really are" is something far greater than trading information about the peculiar particularities of our religious communities and spiritual ways. Dialogue with the others "as they really are" (depth dialogue) is overcoming the fundamental violence: to perceive the other— *a priori*—as less than a sibling, less a child of God than I.

All the great religions acknowledge this equality in the moral realm, the realm of action. So Jesus says: "As you wish that men would do to you, do so to them" (Luke 6:31). Confucius states: "Do not do to others what you would not like yourself" (*Analectic*, XII:2). The Taoist sages say that the good man will regard the gains of others "as if they were his own, and their losses in the same way" (*Thai Shang* 3). Zoroaster says "that nature only is good when it shall not do to another whatever is not good for its own self" (Dadistan—I—dinik, 94:5). In the Mahabharata of Hinduism it is written, "One should never do that to another which one regards as injurious to one's own self..." (*Anushana parva*, 113:7). In the Talmud it is written "What is hateful to yourself do not do to your fellow man" (*Babylonian Talmud*, Shabbath, 31a). And Mohammed writes "No man is a true believer unless he desires for his brother that which he desires for himself" (*Ibn Madja*, Introduction 9).[17] But what is ceded morally, or as cast in moral terms, is regularly denied in theological language by assertions about revelations that seek "universal empire over the souls of men" (H.R. Niebuhr). Thus the moral teaching is obviated and violence endures.

In his important book, *Revelation: the Religious and Violence*, Leo Lefebure says that two factors challenge us to reshape our understanding of revelation. The first is the existence and deepening appreciation of religious traditions other than one's own. The second is "the tragic experience of massive violence and systematic oppression, and the recognition of the historic role of religions in fostering violence and oppression."[18]

It is common to single out Christianity and Islam, the monotheistic religions with the most pronounced missionary impulse in which exclusive claims are most prominent, for pride of place among religions that have generated violence. It is more serviceable, however, to recall the intrinsic ambiguity of all religions. This is one of the implications of the discussion in chapter one of the distinction between spiritual ways and the religious communities in which most of them inhere. A worthy spiritual way is never ambiguous. As proposed earlier, all such ways seek to induce reverence, gratefulness, joy, silence, creativity, courage, justice, forgiveness, compassion and presence to God (or the Ultimate) in praise and penitence.[19]

As for religions, we have not only Pope Urban's *Deus vult*, sanctifying crusader violence. There is more here than Christian and Muslim holy war. As I write, Hindu nationalists in India slay Muslims and Christians, and ultra-orthodox Jews in Israel are forgetful of the Talmudic injunction as it applies to Palestinian Arabs. Even history's most irenic religion can produce this headline: "Monks in Melee: Police Called. Seoul—Monks brandished sticks and smashed collapsible metal chairs on the shaved heads of rival monks yesterday in a leadership dispute within South Korea's largest Buddhist order. At least ten monks and lay people were injured."[20] Much, though not all, of this violence is grounded in absolute claims to exclusively true revelation of God. And the rabid nationalism which is also in play in some instances is bolstered by these claims to exclusive possession of the truth. (The "melee of monks" was over money!)

This is the disaster to which Gabriel Moran, as noted already, refers when he writes "to make revelation into an object of believing has been a disaster."[21] Or, what comes to the same thing, to make the object revealed religion itself. Of this, Wilfred Cantwell Smith writes, "The concept of revelation has been standard in Christian thinking from New Testament time. Yet no one before the eighteenth century...has ever supposed that what was revealed was a religion."[22]

And we can see the continuing influence of such a preposterous notion, as noted in chapter 2, in Paul Bauman's criticism of James Carroll: that the "itch to de-absolutize religion is incompatible with monotheism."[23] In fact this "itch" is at the service of glorifying the Holy One. For what God reveals is not religion but God Godself. And as Rabbi Heschel says "God is either the Father of all men or of no men."[24]

Ruether is right to say that what is at stake in applying the "critical principle" to our religious communities, to their language and social practice, is nothing less than affirming the "full humanity" of all God's children. In a reclaimed theology of revelation, to which we now turn, every human being is known as "the event of God's radical self-communication,"[25] and God Godself as constitutive of every human being's humanity, as *interior intimo meo*, Augustine's God encountered as "nearer to me than I am to myself."[26]

Revelation: Universal, Present, Personal and Responsive

We begin the work of reclaiming an idea of revelation that is worthy of God and does justice to all God's children by repeating Rahner's bold humanistic—indeed, singularly incarnational—assertion that human persons are "the event of God's radical self-communication." Beyond all mythological expression and deeper than anthropomorphic imagery, God is love. Love, or God, loves all that superabundant love has brought into being. At the risk of seeming to patronize the reader, we might nevertheless add this emphasis: all that God's superabundant love has brought into being—which is everything—is loved. And each human person is the "event of God's radical self-communication."

The principal evidence of love is presence—self-communication—to the loved one. (Though its principal expression is probably, as the existential theologians have it, "letting be.")

Franz Rosensweig placed such importance on presence that he writes, in *The Star of Redemption* that "Revelation...is being present itself."[27] And in his masterful translation of the Torah, Everett Fox renders God's answer, in Exodus 3:14, when Moses asks God's name: "I will be there howsoever I will be there...."[28]

Literary figures affirm that love atrophies where presence is diminished. This failure to contemplate the once loved subject is Emily Dickinson's "cobweb on the soul," Eudora Welty's "invisible shadow that falls between people, the veil of indifference to each other's presence, each other's wonder, each other's human plight."[29]

Rahner extends the idea of divine presence and links it to human listening. God speaks and human beings are imbued with the capacity to listen through a "self-transcendence," as he calls it, made possible precisely "through God's ontological and revelatory self-communication."[30] And Gabriel Moran notes "the idea of revelation as present speaking-listening is not a new idea." He calculates that in the Hebrew Bible, for example, there are no fewer than 400 references to God speaking.

Moran is not unmindful of the difficulties traditional religion and traditionally religious people have with the idea of revelation as present speaking and listening. He acknowledges that "the formula that God speaks only in the present may seem a blatant rejection of biblical revelation, Christian doctrine, Church authority and the unsurpassable importance of Jesus of Nazareth." Such fear needs to be addressed in a careful analysis distinguishing revelation and belief. Still, it is from the heart of the mystical tradition itself that we are instructed that revelation is present speaking and listening. Moran writes: "The mystical strand of Christianity affirms the principle that the One who is beyond all names has to be listened for today."[31]

But can it be that despite universal divine love and radical divine self-communication the most loved beings, in order to hear and respond, must cluster together at least in a religious community and, throughout most of the Age of Monologue, not just any religious community but the true one? Rahner answers the question with accustomed profundity (despite the stumble of his idea of "anonymous Christians" and in contradiction of it).

Rahner asks whether revelation (here he uses the term "the supernatural horizon"), can be experienced only from "material which is explicitly religious...only if we use the word 'God,' only if we speak of God's law, only if we explicitly want to do God's will...only if we are involved in an explicitly sacral and religious realm."[32] His answer is no, and it is a quintessentially Catholic theological answer. The capacity to listen, the capacity to respond to God's "radical self-communication," what Rahner here calls every human person's "supernatural elevated transcendentality,"[33] "is also meditated to itself by any and every categorical reality in which and through which the subject becomes present to itself."[34] Rahner concludes "the history of revelation takes place wherever this transcendent history has its history and hence in the whole of human history."[35] To all creation!

In other words, "All the earth praises the Lord."[36] Or, as Roger Haight puts it, "Creation means there is nothing between creation and the creator. God is totally present to creation."[37]

I have tried to establish thus far that what God reveals is God, and that as Love this radical divine self-communication (revelation) is universally available in the mode of reciprocal presence, or what comes to the same thing, speaking and listening in the present. Further, the capacity to listen and respond adequately not only does not require membership in a "true" religion: it does not require membership in any religion.

But this is not yet sufficient bludgeoning of the disastrous idea that revelation can somehow be precisely and timelessly formulated into a content and God circumscribed within a religion. On our way, later in this chapter, to considering both the benefits and liabilities of contents of belief, one further element needs to be added as we seek a reclaimed theology of revelation that does justice to all God's children and is worthy of God. It is the irreducible mystery of God. Elizabeth Johnson gives eloquent voice to this:

> God as God, ground, support and goal of all, is illimitable mystery who, while immanently present, cannot be measured, manipulated or controlled. The doctrine of divine incomprehensibility or hiddenness is a corollary of this divine transcendence. In essence, God's unlikeness to the corporeal and spiritually finite world is total. Hence, human beings simply cannot understand God. No human concept, word or image, all of which originate in experience of created reality, can circumscribe divine reality, nor can any human construct express with any measure of adequacy the mystery of God who is ineffable.[38]

If this isn't clear enough and bracing, or if more classical references are required, consider Augustine: "If you have understood, it is not God." And Thomas Aquinas: "We can know neither God's being nor God's essence."[39]

God, who is the "content" of revelation, is a mystery and ineffable. Rahner goes so far as to say that revelation itself "is the history of the deepening perception of God as the mystery."[40] And Paul Tillich, in a complementary insight, writes, "Whatever is essentially mysterious cannot lose its mystery when it is revealed."[41]

It should be enough to quiet triumphal claims to exclusive and absolute truth to be edified by the faithfulness—the movement toward the Holy—

expressed in the lives of women and men in religious communities on spiritual ways other than one's own. Such witness, if we open ourselves to it, should suffice to quiet untoward claims about revelation if, in humility, we perceive the "others as they really are." But if such witness is insufficient or goes unnoticed, perhaps an appreciation of God's ineffable mystery will empower us to meet one another "our souls...stripped of pretension and conceit...," mindful, in the words of Rabbi Heschel, that "our individual moments of faith are mere waves in the ocean...[and] all formulations and articulations... [are] understatements...."[42]

The preceding remarks pertain chiefly to God and only indirectly to human persons, more to the speaker than to the listener. I hope to have persuaded the reader who needs persuading that God's love mandates that revelation be understood as radical divine self-communication to human persons and that this same love requires universal availability. Further, God's mystery precludes final, absolute, and exclusive codification of revelation as a content owned by a true religion.

To these assertions we must add that revelation is personal; it is received by persons in their aloneness and within communities. "Since acting as a recipient is truly acting and not simply being acted upon, the humans are actively engaged in revelation."[43]

It is a commonplace of the wisdom of religious traditions that revelation entails personal response, a commonplace that often co-exists, oddly, with the contradictory belief in revelation's timelessness. There is, for example, the midrashic question "When was the Torah given...?" The answer: "It is given whenever a person receives it."[44] And writing of an equally time-honored tradition with regard to the Qur'an, Aziz Lahbabi says "Not the text in itself is the revelation but that which the believer discovers every time afresh while reading it."[45]

In contemporary religious thought, we have Rahner's insistence that "there is no proclaimed revelation except in the form of a believed revelation,"[46] and Martin Buber's "Meaning is found through the engagement of one's own person; it only reveals itself as one takes part in the revelation."[47]

Denying the capacity of those who do not belong to the "true religion" to engage fully in divine-human encounter is to deny that the

Holy One communicates to all in unconditioned love. Such a positivist and triumphal stand denies the other's capacity to "welcome in receptivity the self-communication of the divine...," the "form of human experience...," that Roger Haight designates "revelation."[48]

Revelation and Content

To wrest the meaning of revelation from reduction to a content of beliefs, however rich, life-giving, and time-honored the beliefs, appears to be mission impossible. No cavalcade of previously "divinely revealed" beliefs now rightly consigned to the "dustbin of history" (Spinoza) seems adequate against the prereflexive identification of faith and belief. My own modest effort entails changing the nominal form of the former from "faith" to "faithfulness": living in response to God's self-communication.[49] (In this sense divine self-communication and human faithfulness form a continuum as revelation: faithfulness is the human response and therefore constitutive of God's revelation of Godself.) Still, the self-evident historical time and culture bound character of belief remains profoundly elusive. Is it revealed that God "does not wish anyone to perish," as solemnly promulgated at the Ecumenical Council of Arles in 473[50], or, as the Fourth Lateran Council (1215) has it: "Outside the Church no salvation"? Are ecumenical councils the supreme authority in the Church, as the Council of Constance proclaims in 1415, or is the Pope infallible (Vatican Council I, 1869)? Are all the Jews for all times corporately a decide people, as taught for a millennium and more, or are we to follow the Second Vatican Council's repudiation (1962-65) of a belief that was commonplace throughout most of the history of Christianity?

The effort to distinguish faith(fulness) and belief, and thereby liberate revelation from being collapsed to beliefs, has enlisted better men (and women) than I. The effort is crucial if religious language is to cease functioning as an instrument of disputation, exclusive claims and—ultimately—violence. In the early chapters of volume one of *Catholicism*, Richard P. McBrien has an illuminating analysis of the distinction between faith, belief, and theology. In an equally compelling piece, his 1986 essay, "The Meaning of Faith in Relation to

Justice,"[51] Avery Dulles sets out a threefold idea of faithfulness as assensual, fiducial, and performative, that is, convictions affirmed by intellectual assent, trusting feelings toward God affirmed in prayer and, thirdly, action to heal the world and its people. As perhaps the most prolific and profoundly neo-orthodox Catholic theologian of our times, Cardinal Dulles is known to impute great authority to traditional patterns of belief, authoritatively held, that is to the "content" of belief sometimes called the "deposit of faith" [sic] (what is really the content or deposit of doctrinally, and sometimes dogmatically, held beliefs). Yet, even Dulles can write "The true content of revelation is the divinely intended and humanly perceived significance of the events and words."[52] Which comes down to saying revelation is vivid personal experience in the present.

Still, religious beliefs are obviously intrinsic to religious communities and uphold spiritual paths. The great patristics and liturgy scholar Joseph Andreas Jungmann played a pivotal role in shifting Catholic religious education from "arid intellectualism" by calling for practice that was scriptural and liturgical with an attendant emphasis on experience. But Jungmann could also write that "Knowledge must furnish light for desire."[53] There is, in other words, no effort here to dismiss or even relegate the importance of content of belief to persons and the religious communities they inhabit in insisting that we distinguish faith(fulness) and beliefs. There is only the desire to protect the rich and vital experience of God in present experience from encapsulation in limited creedal formulations. And there is the desire to frame our theological language about faith(fulness) and belief—their relationship and their differentness—in a fashion that acknowledges all God's children as participating (to use Rahner's phrase again) in "supernatural elevated transcendentality," that is, as grounded in God and fully open to divine-human relationship.

It is certainly instructive to ask and answer the question why the distinction between revelation and content of beliefs is so difficult to grasp. It is also important to ask and answer why the distinction is resisted by some who know the difference. As to the first question, at least three causes come to mind.

1. Human beings by and large crave certitude, in a Christian context what Franz Joseph von Beeck, SJ, calls the problem of "objectivity" in "Christian faith."[54]

2. Many members of many religions, perhaps most members of most religions, to some extent fear what Leonard Swidler calls the "deabsolutizing influences (relativism) of patterns of thinking and acting in the modern world."[55]

3. Built into many, perhaps most, religions is the imperative to make absolute truth claims, what Rabbi Heschel's calls "the inherent weakness," of religion in segregating God. And there are other causes.

In an essay in *Theological Studies*, Franz Joseph Von Beeck cites "the problem [of]...supernatural divine revelation...[as]...the principal intellectual challenge...offered to Christianity...[in]...the modern era."[56] This is the problem of "objectivity" referred to above. The problem is of relatively modern origin according to von Beeck, who speaks of "the first half of the sixteenth century which witnessed the rise of the cultivation of 'objectivity' as never before."[57] If, as Von Beeck counsels, we return to the theology of the Fathers we are delivered from what he calls a "crude interventionism"[58] in understanding divine activity. We are, von Beeck asserts, delivered from the reduction of the mystery of "God's ongoing self-communication to humanity," to "a 'deposit' of absolute truths, inaccessible to reason by definition and hence acceptable only by God-given faith upon the sole authority of the magisterium...."[59] He continues:

> The Church Fathers' notion of God's activity in the world is not rooted in a naïve...conception of effective causation on the part of God in relation to particular occurrences. Instead the Fathers place all divine action in the world in the context of an understanding of divine immanence, an understanding in which the human person plays a decisive role.[60]

Von Beeck sights a number of Church Fathers exemplary of which are Irenaeus' insistence, in *Against Heresy*, that God's immanence is so utter that "God does not need to break in to enter," and Gregory of Nyssa: "The divine is equally in all and it permeates the whole of creation in the same way...."[61]

This is being written in the midst of what is uniformly being called the "clergy sexual abuse scandal" in the Catholic Church, a crisis that might more accurately be called the crisis of "unworthy leadership and sexual abuse" in the Church. One may reasonably ask whether the yearning for "objectivity" in "Christian faith" that gives rise to the disastrous collapse of revelation and beliefs is especially prominent among those who are credited as authoritative keepers of a "deposit" of truths which is complete (or "full"). Lay Catholics in the United States urge a revisiting of early traditions of belief and practice in the Church in which, for example, bishops were chosen by local communities, clerical celibacy was not yet mandated universally in the West and, briefly but significantly, women played authoritative roles in formative times.

Many Catholic hierarchs, creatures of a restorationist papacy to which the strategy of welding a fundamentalism of dogma comes readily, regularly invoke "revealed truths." Many dissenting but loyal lay Catholics, on the other hand, rest their arguments not only on retrieving lost traditions but on the development of doctrine and on revelation in the "signs of the times." In doing so, they avoid disastrous association of revelation with static, current practice, often framed and justified without reference to a broader history of practice.

A particularly arresting example of how this all works was provided by Cardinal Bernard Law. Speaking to youth at World Youth Day in Toronto in Summer, 2002, Law responded to a question about women's ordination:

It [women's ordination] is one of the things I don't think about, because it can't change. I know it can't change, I know it won't change, and I know to be thinking in those terms is to deceive oneself and to waste one's energy....Jesus established this order of service and it has been an unbroken tradition....Just rest comfortably in the faith and understand that this has nothing to do about equality.[62]

How is it possible to read such a thing, in such a context, and not affirm H. Richard Niebuhr's insight that "A theology of revelation...may direct attention away from the God visible in the community....the idea of revelation itself may be employed not for the greater glory of God but as a weapon for the defense and aggrandizement of the Church."[63]

The second, related, difficulty in distinguishing revelation and beliefs (along with the search for objectivity), is fear of "deabsolutizing influences" in the modern world, that is, fear of relativism. It is a matter to which some considerable attention was given earlier. But it is worth visiting again in our discussion of revelation.

Leonard Swidler identifies six deabsolutizing influences: 1. historicism, 2. intentionality analysis, 3. sociology of knowledge, 4. a recognition of the limits of knowledge, 5. modern hermeneutics or interpretation theory, and 6. dialogue itself. These deabsolutizing influences cause resistance to pluralism based on fear of relativism. The fear leads to the retrenchment of restoration. And restoration makes ample use of a kind of dogmatics like that implied in Cardinal Law's dismissal of the possibility of the ordination of women, the kind of use of a language of dogmatic finality so fundamentalist that it moves Garry Wills to say, of these kinds of assertions, that they "would make a sophomore blush."[64]

In front of the fear of relativism and the fundamentalist absolutism which it engenders, we can only rest again in the wisdom of H. Richard Niebuhr: "It is not evident that the man who is forced to confess that his view oft is conditioned by the standpoint he occupies must doubt the reality of what he sees."[65]

This sense of the "reality of what [one] sees," is one of the glories of the Catholic intellectual-theological stream in the history of Christian thought. And we should not take leave of the topic of "revelation and content" without noting again the importance of intellectual assent to convictions, convictions that are enshrined in beliefs and sometimes elevated to doctrine or dogma, in Catholic traditions. For the importance of this element is not under siege here.

In a seminal work on Catholicism, the Baptist theologian Landon Gilkey writes this of the Catholic genius for honoring the intellectual content of belief:

> ...there has been throughout Catholic history a drive toward rationality, the insistence that the divine mystery manifest in tradition and sacramental presence be in so far as possible penetrated, defended, and explicated by the most acute rational reflection. The value of this traditional insistence in an age concerned with

cognitive certainty and reflective clarity is undoubted, and is one of the main reasons that Catholicism has such an important role to play in the Christian future.[66]

At its very best the Catholic tradition of honoring an intelligible and broadly continuous content of belief, a tradition richly summed up in Anselm's definition of theology as *fides quarens intellectum*, "faith seeking understanding," is Christianity's strongest bulwark against "fideism": the pernicious idea that faithfulness requires the *sacrificium intellectum*, the "sacrifice of the mind." It is, however, precisely this contribution that is rescinded when officials within the Catholic Church revert to a neo-fundamentalism of doctrine, a static or "classicist" interpretation and teaching which denies the obvious historical evidence of change and development, corruption and reform. This is something officials do out of fear of modernity or for reasons of their own self-interest. When we pretend that nothing changes or develops, we forget Newman's great insight that these elements are ever-present: "In a higher world it is otherwise, but here below to live is to change and to be perfect is to have changed often."[67]

The challenge, the richness, the acute theological workmanship entailed in preserving and extending the Catholic intellectual-theological tradition is captured by Karl Rahner. One can almost feel Rahner's anxious care that, on the one hand, patterns of traditional belief are preserved and renewed, and on the other that the mystery of the Holy One present to us is not squandered. Rahner writes:

> The clearest formulations, the most sanctified formulas, the classic condensations of the centuries—long work of the Church in prayer, reflection and struggle concerning God's mysteries: all these derive their life from the fact that they are not an end but a beginning, not a goal but a means, truths which open the way to the—ever greater—Truth....Every formula transcends itself...not because it is false but precisely because it is true.[68]

Rahner's is really a more traditional mindset than that of ultra-traditionalists. And like him, Van Beeck and Richard P. McBrien see the neo-fundamentalist handling of the content of belief as a product of a later fear of modernity. McBrien ascribes it to "the new rationalist climate of the sixteenth and seventeenth centuries," and the rise of a "new and more rigid scholasticism" under the influence of which "defenders of traditional Christian faith became more inflexible."[69]

And Gabriel Moran links the rise of a static notion of revelation, seen as an objective content of belief, to our forgetting and displacing the dynamism of Aquinas' approach:

> "Doctrina" for Aquinas means teaching...the reception of that teaching is "disciplina"....For both Aquinas and Aristotle teaching-learning is a single process....Revelation for Aquinas is a case of good teaching and human learning. But just as the word "doctrine" migrated from action to content, "revelation" came to refer to a what, the object grasped in the human reception.[70]

The importance of a body of convictions or beliefs for individuals and religious communities is really self-evident. But God's self-communication is relational, experiential, and present. And people in religious communities grow in faithfulness by retrieving lost traditions of belief and practice and by responding to the Holy Spirit in the signs of the times. To do this we must resist conflating revelation and belief, and we must resist the specious claim that the beliefs are timeless and unchanging. To the question: "What is revelation?" we must answer "It is no thing. Revelation is not a content that can be contained anywhere. It is a present and living relation between the divine and the human."[71]

We must avoid identifying revelation and beliefs in order to cultivate a sensitivity to the faithfulness of these "others" in our midst, a reverential appreciation for women and men in other religious communities and other spiritual paths. Then we will recognize these siblings as, like us, capable (to employ Roger Haight's words again) of "welcom[ing] in receptivity the self-communication of the divine...." But the distinction between revelation and belief breaks down. And members of one or another triumphal religious institution will wander, blind and dangerous, never noticing that these "others" too grow in reverence, gratefulness, joy, silence, courage, creativity, justice, forgiveness, compassion and praise and penitence before the Holy One.

Revelation and Practice

Gabriel Moran writes:

> If "revelation" is assumed to be theoretical knowledge that is the
> unveiling of an object which is gazed upon, then the practice of a
> religious way of life begins with a separation of beliefs and prac-
> tices. In contrast, if revelation is itself practical, emerging only as
> one practices the religion, then the moral life, intellectual under-
> standing and education in religion take on different shapes.[72]

For a reclaimed notion of revelation worthy of God and reverential
toward siblings on spiritual ways and in religious communities other
than one's own, the practical evidence of revelation (the presence of
God), must be taken with great seriousness. Revelation is manifest in
practice. The capacity to respond in gratitude to the self-communication of the Holy One is bolstered by convictions, and the faithful are
consoled, amidst life's suffering and sorrows, by prayer, dimensions
that parallel Dulles' idea of assensual and fiducial layers of faithfulness.

But the proof that beliefs are not illusory or prayer merely with-
drawal will be attested by the practice of works of justice and of peace.
This is what Dulles refers to as the "performative" layer of faithfulness.
The practical character of revelation, in this sense, is brought home
with special clarity, and not a little humor, in a remarkable confessional essay by John Hicks, the renowned theologian of religious pluralism. The essay, entitled "A Pluralist View," appears in a collection
entitled *More Than One Way? Four Views of Salvation in a Pluralist
World*.

Hicks says "I began my Christian life as a fundamentalist."[73]
However, during fifteen years, living and working in Birmingham,
England, he engaged in a great deal of "community organization":

> I went frequently to Jewish synagogues, Muslim mosques, Sikh
> guruwaras, Hindu temples, and, of course, a variety of churches.
> In these places of worship I soon realized something that is obvi-
> ous enough once noticed, yet momentous in its implications. This
> is that although the language, concepts, liturgical actions, and cul-
> tural ethos differ widely from one another, yet from a religious
> point of view basically the same thing is going on in all of them,

namely, human beings coming together within the framework of an ancient and highly developed tradition to open their hearts and minds to God, whom they believe makes a total claim on their lives and demands of them, in the words of one of the prophets, "to do justice, and to love kindness, and to walk humbly with your God." (Micah 6:8)

And then the coup de grace:

But is this what we would expect if Christians have a more complete and direct access to God than anyone else and live in a closer relationship to him, being indwelt by the Holy Spirit? Should not the fruits of the Spirit, which according to St. Paul are "love, joy, peace, patience, kindness, goodness, faithfulness, gentleness. self-control" (Gal 5:22–23) be more evident in Christian than in non-Christian lives? It would not, of course, be fair to expect that any randomly selected Christian be morally superior to any randomly selected non-Christian. But surely the average level of these virtues should be noticeably higher among Christian than among non-Christians. But it does not seem to me that in fact Christians are on average noticeably morally superior to Jews, Muslims, Hindus, Sikhs, or Buddhists. Rather than suggest a comparative quantification of a kind that is in fact not possible, I propose the more modest and negative conclusion: that it is not possible to establish the moral superiority of the adherents of any one of the great traditions over the rest.

And Hicks has one more bit of work dismantling religious triumphalism based on claims of revelation. He insists that authentic revelation results in elevated moral practice, which is itself the concrete expression of salvation. But, "A conservative," he says "might be tempted to reply [to what Hicks is quoted saying above] that morality is something different from salvation."

But is such a reply adequate? If we define salvation as an actual human change, a gradual transformation from natural self-centeredness (with all the human evils that flow from it) to a radical new orientation centered in God and manifest in the "fruits of the Spirit," then it seems clear that salvation is taking place within all the world's religions—and taking place, so far as we can tell, to more or less the same extent. On this view, which is not based on theological theory but on observable realities of human life, salvation is not a juridical transaction inscribed in heaven, nor is it a future hope beyond this life (although it is this too), but it is a spiritual, moral and political change that can begin now and whose present possibility is grounded in the structure of reality.

Revelation, God Godself, is available to all that divine love has brought into existence. In chapter four we treat an appreciation of revelation lived by those who are "other" for us, a deeper appreciation of Christian faithfulness by Jewish and other readers as a case in point of emerging reverence across different religious communities, different spiritual paths.

Notes

1. Chapter two, page 57.
2. Chapter one, p. 10.
3. Swidler, op. cit., p. 41.
4. H. Richard Niebuhr, *The Meaning of Revelation* (London: Macmillian Company, 1970).
5. Krister Stendahl in personal conversation.
6. Gregory Baum, *Religion and Alienation: A Theological Reading of Sociology* (New York: Paulist Press, 1975). See Chapter IX, "Critical Theology."
7. Donald Dietrich, "The Need For a Critique of the Institutional Church," *Catholics, Jews, and the Prism of Conscience: A Response to James Carroll's Book Constantine's Sword* (Waltham, MA: Brandeis University Office of Public Affairs, 2001).
8. Chapter two, p. 44.
9. Leo. D. Lefebure, *Revelation, the Religions, and Violence* (Maryknoll, NY: Orbis Press, 2001), p. 108.
10. It is the full humanity of others, whether they too are intimately linked to the Holy One, which is brought into question when exclusive truth claims relegate persons in religious communities other than one's own to a status less than one's own in the eye of God.

11. Rosemary Radford Ruether, *Sexism and God-Talk: Toward a Feminist Theology* (Boston: Beacon Press, 1983), p. 18f.

12. Ibid., p. 23.

13. Niebuhr, op. cit., p 29.

14. McBrien, op.cit., p. 242.

15. From "The Nichomachean Ethics," Books 7 and 9. Cited in Robert Bellah, Richard Madsen, William Sullivan, Ann Swidler, Steven M. Tipton, *Habits of the Heart:: Individualism and Commitment in American Life* (Berkeley: University of California Press, 1985), p. 115.

16. Wiggins, op. cit., p. 6.

17. John Hicks, "A Pluralist View" in Denis l. Okholm and Timothy R. Phillips (eds.), *More Than One Way? Four Views on Salvation in a Pluralist World* (Grand Rapids: Zondervan Publishing House, 1995), p. 39f.

18. Lefebure, op. cit., p. 6.

19. Chapter two, p. 49.

20. Reported in the *Boston Globe.*, November 11, 1999.

21. Chapter two, p. 52.

22. Quoted in Moran, *Both Sides*, op. cit., p. 86.

23. Chapter two, p. 41.

24. S. Heschel, op. cit., p. 398.

25. Rahner, *Foundations*, op. cit., p. 126.

26. St. Augustine, *The Confessions*, Chapter 3.

27. Quoted in Moran, *Both Sides*, op. cit., p. 128.

28. Fox, op. cit., p. 273.

29. Emily Dickinson is quoted in Margaret Farley, *Personal Commitments: Beginning, Keeping, Changing* (San Franciso: Harper and Row, 1986), p. 56. Eudora Welty is quoted in the *New York Times*, July 24, 2001.

30. Rahner, *Foundations*, op. cit., p. 153.

31. The references to God speaking in the Hebrew Bible are from Moran, *Both Sides*, op. cit., p. 25; and to the "mystical strand" from p. 75.

32. Rahner, *Foundations*, op.cit., p. 151.

33. We might call it being a child of God and paying attention.

34. Rahner, *Foundations*, op. cit., p. 151.

35. Ibid., p. 153.

36. Psalm 148.

37. Roger Haight, *Jesus, Symbol of God*. (Maryknoll, NY: Orbis Press, 2000), p. 193.

38. Elizabeth Johnson, *She Who Is: The Mystery of God in Feminist Theological Discourse* (New York: Crossroad, 1993), p. 104f.

39. Augustine sermon 117 and Aquinas in ST 1 q. 3, a.4 both quoted in Jacques Dupuis, SJ, *Toward a Christian Theology of Religious Pluralism* (Maryknoll, NY: Orbis Press, 2000), p. 242.

40. Cited in Johnson, op. cit., p. 105. (From *Theological Investigations*, volume 16.)

41. Tillich, op. cit., p. 109 (vol. 1).

42. See chapter two, note 17.

43. Moran, *Both Sides*, op. cit., p. 134.

44. Ibid., p. 21, cited from *What is Judaism?*

45. Ibid., p.228, cited from *Deciphering the Signs of God*.

46. Ibid., p. 122. From "What is a Dogmatic Statement?" *Theological Investigations*, volume V.

47. Ibid., p. 125, from *The Eclipse of God*.

48. Haight, op. cit., p. 193.

49. O'Hare, *Faithfulness*, op. cit.

50. Knitter, *No Other*, op. cit., p. 122.

51. Avery Dulles, "The Meaning of Faith Considered in Relationship to Justice," in John Haughey, SJ (ed), *The Faith That Does Justice* (New York: Paulist Press, 1977), pp. 10 to 46.

52. Quoted in McBrien, op. cit., p. 252.

53. Joseph Andreas Jungmann, *The Good News Yesterday and Today* (New York: Sadlier Company, 1962), p. 8. The twenty-fifth anniversary edition, originally published as *The Good News and Our Proclamation of the Faith*.

54. Franz Joseph von Beeck, "Divine Revelation: Intervention of Self-Communication," *Theological Studies*, June 1991, vol 52, no. 2, p. 198.

55. Leonard Swidler, *After the Absolute: The Dialogical Future of Religious Reflection* (Minneapolis: Fortress Press, 1990).

56. Ibid., p. 199.

57. Ibid., p. 205.

58. Ibid., p. 203.

59. Ibid., p. 224.

60. Ibid., p. 204.

61. Ibid.

62. Michael Paulson, "Law Affirms Church Doctrine to Youth," the *Boston Globe*, vol. 262, no. 27, July 27, 2002, p. A7.

63. Niebuhr, op. cit., p. 28.

64. Wills, op. cit., p. 5.

65. Niebuhr, op. cit., p. 13.

66. Langdon Gilkey, *Catholicism Confronts Modernity: A Protestant View* (New York: Seabury Press, 1975), p. 22f.

67. Cited from "An Essay on the Development of Doctrine," in Garry Wills, *Why I Am a Catholic* (New York: Houghton Mifflin Company, 2002) p. 285.

68. Rahner, *Investigations*, op. cit., p. 148f. Cited earlier in chapter 2; see note 28.

69. McBrien, op. cit, p. 242.

70. Cited in Moran, *Both Sides*, op. cit., p. 71.

71. Ibid., p. 18.

72. Ibid., p. 47.

73. All quotes of John Hicks are from Okholm and Phillips, op. cit., 29–43.

CHAPTER FOUR

How Reverence Emerges

This chapter takes its name from the sentiment expressed in chapter two, that when we "see and understand the convictions of the other as illuminating common religious experiences, then we recognize the other as a companion...on...a journey of compassion, a fellow traveler on this earth." We experience greater reverence for the other.

The chapter tests the idea, first noted in chapter one, of the "possible complimentarity of theological dialogue and spiritual companionship." The discussion in this chapter of the liberal Christian theological consensus (used interchangeably hereafter with the term "Catholic spirit" and sometimes as the "liberal Christian theological consensus"), engages us in theological discourse. But when we turn at the end of the chapter to the life and thought of Thomas Merton, we move, as I noted earlier, from theology to "depth theology." This parallels what I did in my 1997 book, *The Enduring Covenant: The Education of Christians and the End of Antisemitism*, where the movement was from an interpretation of features of Jewish theological and moral conviction to a profile of a witness (Abraham Joshua Heschel) embodying its spiritual genius. Here Merton exemplifies faithfulness in a Christian key to the human vocation: living well and striving to be like God.

Church, Officialdom, and Catholic Spirit

The liberal Christian theological consensus on the Church, introduced briefly in chapter two, is that its essential characteristic is that it is a community, or more precisely a community of communities with federated institutional links.[1] Even where hierarchy is present, it is viewed as a function for the service of people within the community and not, itself, the definitive feature of the Church. In this, liberal Christianity is akin to Judaism in its most richly communal expression.

In fact, however, Catholic and some other institutional expressions of Christianity are pervasively and definitively hierarchical with a comparatively small number of authoritarian figures wielding power. Moran writes of this: "Everyone outside the Catholic Church knows very well that the church is a power structure and that blithely to dismiss the fact is an abuse of language and an affirmation of unchecked power."[2] After a short period of time in which a communal model of the church was prominent, Catholic officialdom sought successfully during the pontificate of Pope John Paul II, since 1978, to reassert a more hierarchic view and practice. I proposed in chapter two that their efforts have brought renewed prominence to legalism, abridgement of intellectual freedom, authoritarianism, a specious traditionalism, exclusivism, and focus on a Christ triumphant of which Christian scripture knows little.

Ten years out from the close of the reformist Second Vatican Council in 1975, but three years before the commencement of the pontificate of John Paul II, Karl Rahner captured the state of affairs: "The Church's public life even today (for all the good will which is not to be questioned) is dominated to a terrifying extent by ritualism, legalism, administration and a boring and resigned spiritual mediocrity continuing along familiar lines."[3]

As a power structure, the Church has done terrible things through the centuries alongside many spiritually, morally, and culturally enriching things. I don't think it is anachronistic to say of relations between the Church and the Jewish people during these centuries that they are history's most instructive case of the evil of religion as power structure. Two examples, drawn from recent times but exemplifying much through the centuries, illustrate my point. John Cornwell's book, *Hitler's Pope*, demonstrates that in the papal march to centralized Vatican control over the worldwide Church, abetting the ascendancy of the Nazi party in Germany in the early 1930s was not too great a price to pay.[4] And Robert Kertzer's book, *The Pope Against the Jews*, shows that antisemitism became a focused Vatican strategy in the late nineteenth and early twentieth centuries to forestall its loss of temporal power because "the same forces that had struck against the power of the Church had guaranteed the Jews equal rights....Jews could be used to discredit the forces that had sought to create the modern secular state."[5]

The origins of how the Catholic Church got to be such a power structure are traceable to its fourth-century legitimation, but also manipulation, by the Emperor Constantine. This is an historical pivot point, energizing both the worldwide spread of the message of Jesus Christ and the growth of a great power structure with all the corrupting influences noted above. Paula Fredrickson asks how, within only a few decades of being decriminalized and recognized as the official religion of the Roman Empire, "Christians [could] come so readily to avail themselves of the powers of coercion," given the irenic origins of the Jesus movement. Her stark answer: the fourth century is really "the period of the conversion not of Constantine but of Christianity."[6] And James Carroll says "There are few things we can say with more certainty about Jesus than that he defined his mission in opposition not to Judaism but to the imperium of Rome....But the Church has never truly come to terms with the contradiction it embraced when the Roman imperium and Roman Catholicism became the same thing."[7]

None of which is to say that a kind of hierarchy, or the right kind of hierarchy, cannot exist richly within a communal model of the Church. Examples, spanning the centuries, are Augustine of Hippo and Pope John XXIII.

Garry Wills has made it a grail of sorts to reintroduce Augustine's genius, his life and work, to contemporary readers, as noted in chapter two. The greatest of the Western Fathers of the Patristic period,

Augustine's influence is profound and enduring. As a bishop in North Africa in the sixth century, he was a model, as Wills shows, of communal sensitivity. Faced with scandals in the local church, he acted with complete openness, inviting scrutiny, including lay participants in a tribunal he convened to handle a controversy over disputed property and other matters, and reporting results of his investigation as soon as they became available.[8]

In turning to the twentieth-century example of Pope John XXIII, it is important to note that virtually every feature of restored triumphal hierarchy to which reference has been made impinges negatively on women in church and in society. From this different kind of hierarch, Pope John XXIII, however, we read in the encyclical *Pacem in Terris*, ("Peace on Earth"): "Since women are becoming ever more conscious of their human dignity, they will not tolerate being treated as mere material instruments but demand rights befitting a human person in both domestic and public life."[9]

Triumphal hierarchy needs to be moralistic. As Johannes Metz writes, if the Church is not "radical," in the sense of hewing sincerely to the purity of the message of Jesus Christ, it must mask its short-fall of idealism with a veneer of "rigorism."[10] James Carroll picks up this theme in an essay titled "Redefining the 'Bad Catholic.'"[11] Of the legalistic division of Catholics into "good" and "bad," Carroll writes "at bottom, the division's real purpose was to protect the pyramidal authority structure of hierarchy."[12]

The easy and apodictic distinction between good and bad Catholics is blessedly blurring even while the grounds for judgments thereof shift and broaden. Though Carroll employs the past tense, there are plenty among neo-fundamentalist Catholics today for whom all is still quite clear:

> You could be excommunicated for having an abortion—but not for being a Nazi. You could be homosexual in the Church but not in a public way....You could remarry after divorce, but only if your divorce could be labeled an "annulment." You could practice birth control, but only the method deemed "natural." The Church controlled the inner lives of Catholics by making the sexual ethos the

one area of moral absolutism. That is why abortion still trumps the death penalty...,why condoms draw Church fire and napalm doesn't.[13]

Carroll concludes that "As the girder of a power structure, the system was ingenuous, because sexual restlessness defines the human condition."[14]

The perennial Manichean treatment of sexuality by the Catholic Church is instructive for distinguishing official Church from Catholic spirit. The Catholic spirit, the whole liberal Christian consensus, in addition to being deeply communal, is profoundly humanistic. It affirms all that is human, taking as its motto Irenaeus' second-century anthem *Gloria Dei vivens homo*, the "glory of God is humans fully alive." Writing of this spirit, the Baptist theologian Langdon Gilkey, while cautioning that "the official and objective structure of Catholicism still reflects an anti-natural, anti-sensual, moralistic...view of general human existence,"[15] also says "Catholic life itself...reflects a freedom from moralistic prohibitions and judgments...[and] has a continued experience unequaled in other forms of Christianity of the presence of God and grace mediated through symbols to the entire course of ordinary human life...of transcendent mystery impinging continually on human existence."[16] In this, the liberal Christian theological consensus (or the Catholic spirit) mirrors the Judaism to which it is indebted. We can see this in Milton Steinberg's observation that "the tension between body and soul which so harrowed first the pagan world and then the Christian is relaxed in Judaism."[17] For whereas "Dualism despairs in advance of half of reality and half of human nature...,Judaism holds that there is nothing that cannot be retrieved for the good."[18]

This shared humanistic allegiance arises from the fact that in both healthy Judaism and the liberal Christian consensus the goal is the sanctification of life and not a feverish program for achieving individual salvation. It is certainly true, as Jacob Neusner, among others,[19] has proposed, that an official Catholicism (or an official Christianity) is occupied with a specific rendition of the salvation of the world, whereas Judaism is for the sanctification of Israel and the world. But the Catholic spirit, the liberal Christian agenda, like the Judaism it emulates, is deeply "sacramental." In this perspective, "one 'sees' the divine in the human, the infinite in the finite, the spiritual in the material, the transcendent in the immanent, the eternal in the historical....Therefore, all reality is sacred."[20] For those influenced by the sacramental imagination, salvation and sanctification, heaven and earth, are united. As Rosemary Haughton puts it: "What I regard as the theological basis of the Catholic enterprise is the attempt to carry out the job of loving everything on earth to the point where earth becomes heaven."[21]

Returning to Judaism and liberal Christianity's shared affinity for the communal, we note with Richard McBrien that the value cuts in another direction beside rejecting triumphal hierarchy. It also rejects individualism in religious and social life. McBrien names "sacramentality," "meditation," and "communion" the three defining principles of the Catholic spirit. Of communion, he writes: "Our way to God and God's way to us is...a communal way. Even when the divine-human encounter is most personal and individual it is still communal, in that the encounter is made possible by the meditation of a community of faith...."[22]

The preference for communality over triumphal hierarchy makes the conversation about the democratization of the Church inevitable. But as James Carroll says, to say "democracy" is to employ that "most ecclesiatically incorrect word of all...."[23]

A common place of communal Judaism is expressed in good-natured jokes about "two Jews and three synagogues," or harried congregational rabbis contending with assertive lay synagogue leadership, or by the whimsical answer to the question, "Who speaks for the Jews?" What lies below this doggerel is the fact of a basic democracy attaching to even much traditional Orthodox Judaism. If this value is common in Judaism, it is rare in official Christianity of any denomination. And on the difference between triumphal hierarchy and democracy in the churches rests nothing less—again the word is James Carroll's—than whether life in the religious community is a "liberation" or an "infantilization." Gabriel Moran nails the fact that these are simply the only options. Writing precisely of this topic, the democratization of the Church, Moran says "I use democratic as the only alternative to authoritarian....Authoritarian refers to a unilateral exercise of power in which someone has the right to command and other people have the duty to obey. Democratic refers to a mode of interaction in which authority is grounded in exchange of power so that power is not absolutized anywhere."[24]

It matters at two levels that a communal and humanistic view and practice of Church life regain ascendancy among Christians. Negatively, it matters because an authoritarian and triumphal church is always primed to encourage a religiously inspired xenophobia which its officials may formally reject but still instigate among ultra-conservative confessants. (In this sense, as I implied with the vignette that opened chapter two, there are few if any strictly intramural Church issues.)

More positively, one hopes the appreciation of their shared view of their religions as properly communal and humanistic will move some Jews and Christians to deeper spiritual encounter. The hope extends as well to any pairing of peoples in two religious communities who become aware of such values shared one with the other.

The Doctrine of Christ

In *Judaism and Christianity*, Leo Baeck wrote of Jesus "We behold a man who is Jewish in every feature of his character, manifesting in every particular what is pure and good in Judaism. This man could have developed as he came to be only on the soil of Judaism; and only on this soil too could be found disciples and followers....Here alone, in this Jewish sphere, in this Jewish atmosphere...could this man live his life and meet his death, a Jew among Jews."[25]

The importance of recovering and appreciating the Jewishness of Jesus and of the early Christian movement cannot be overstated. But there is a deeper level at which some Jews and Christians of the liberal theological consensus can encounter, even in the doctrine of Christ, a common value and religious experience. This is the shared incarnationalism of both Judaism and Christianity. Of it, Eliot Wolfson writes "the idea of incarnation unique to Christianity should be viewed as a 'particular framing' of the conception of incarnation that was idiomatic to a variety of Jewish authors who represent God as a person."[26]

A great deal of ground clearing is needed, however, before recognition of our shared incarnational spirit frees some Jews and Christians of the liberal theological consensus to recognize one another and support one another more fully on the spiritual journey. As I noted earlier, a good deal of dogmatic positivism and naïve realism hides the common experience and symbolic meaning of religious language developed over centuries in our different religious communities. The dominant "particular framing" of the doctrines of christology over these many centuries is such that the incarnational inheritance is virtually limited to Jesus of Nazareth; all others, and especially the unbaptized, are alienated from this gift. The language of belief, which is analogical and metaphorically rich, is taken to designate and describe precise physical realities and a further wedge is opened between doctrinal claims about the incarnation of God in Jesus of Nazareth and the common human incarnational vocation and inheritance evoked in every religious community that shares this spirit.

So before we return to Wolfson's thesis, in his essay "Judaism and Incarnation," we need to appreciate more fully the symbolic character of the "particular framing" of Christian incarnationalism. And for this we cannot do better than be led by Roger Haight and his superb study, *Jesus, Symbol of God.*[27]

Haight sets out six characteristics of religious symbols. They: 1. demand participation; 2. mediate meaning by activating the mind; 3. point to the transcendent; 4. reveal the essence of human existence; 5. are multivalent, possessing more than one meaning; and 6. are dialectical; they entail a creative tension of seeming opposites. (On the last characteristic, Haight notes, for example, that a sacred stone remains a stone.)

In each of these dimensions, Jesus Christ is, for Christians, symbol of God. Or, we might substitute for "symbol of God" (without altering the meaning of the phrase), "revelation of God," or "makes the Divine present."[28] For those for whom he so functions, Jesus Christ brings the divine and human closer; the "spirit" in meat (*carne*) or materiality, in other words, incarnation. And Jesus Christ is experienced by Christians as enabling salvation, salvation, as Haight following Peter

Abelard says, "not as payment but... [as]...love."[29] As teacher, Jesus Christ reveals for some the story of God as loving creator overcoming the bondage of human existence to evil. As himself faithful to the human vocation, Jesus Christ mediates for some the experience of divine fidelity. As risen, for some, Jesus Christ fulfills the "promise that meets the hope of human existence."[30]

But precisely how, for some, is God—the Divine—"revealed," "present," "in" Jesus Christ? The answer is: existentially. God embodied, revealed and present in Jesus Christ existentially: "God did not act through Jesus in historically empirical ways."[31] The Divine revelation or presence is symbolic and "symbolic communication is not objective in the sense that it can be accomplished without subjective or existential engagement in that which is being communicated."[32] "Faith is primarily an elemental, existential human response."[33]

We return to Elliott Wolfson's "thesis that classical Jewish sources yield a philosophical [sic] conception of incarnation...."[34] The divine is incarnate in prayer and study, in the "man" with whom Jacob struggles and with whom he comes "face to face" (Gen 32:30), in the "indwelling of glory in the tabernacle,"[35] in the Temple, in the sanctuary and in the many "incarnations of the divine in the angelic figure...in passages where there is a deliberate confusion between the Angel of God and divinity itself."[36] And, finally, "Just as early Christian exegetes saw in Christ God made flesh so the rabbis conceived of the Torah as the incarnation of the image of God...the Shechinah dwells among ten men who sit together occupied with the Torah, as it says 'God stands in the divine assembly (Ps 82:1).'"[37] All of which prompts Wolfson to conclude "In the end the christological doctrine of incarnation is not, as Paul surmised, a stumbling block particular to the Jews, but rather to anyone whose religious sensibility has not been properly nourished by the well springs of poetic imagination."[38]

Wolfson highlights a crucial distinction between the Jewish incarnationalism which he is treating and the "particular framing" of incarnation that has, regrettably, achieved classical status in the "high," metaphysical christologies which still predominate in Christian life. He says of all these Jewish incarnations that they are "docetic," that is "semblances" (as he translates the Greek *dokesei*) of the divine. Sadly, the hole into which classical christology has fallen over the centuries is to embrace a docetic interpretation but one in which Jesus Christ is not so much "semblance" (or symbol) of God. Classical christology features a doceticism in which, functionally, Jesus' humanity is only a semblance and Jesus and God are utterly conflated.

We Jews and Christians have a better shot at spiritual companionship around our common incarnational feature if Christian docetism can be shed. And the principal way to do this is to insist that christology is about God, not properly the catalogue of what were called "metaphysical conceits" built up around the person of Jesus Christ. In this regard, Haight assures us that the primitive Christian community preserved its own focus on God. He says that "the Christian community relates to [Jesus] as to a heavenly being. But he is not portrayed as God with a cult of his own."[39] And Bernard Cooke, in his influential study of Jesus' experience of God as "Abba," writes "Jesus' teaching was entirely occupied with witnessing to the reality of his Abba and contained practically nothing about himself except by way of implication."[40]

In contrast, it is common to bolster docetic christology by reference to "Logos" or "Word" christology especially found in the last canonical gospel, the Gospel of John, with its dramatic opening portrayal of Jesus Christ as the pre-existent Word (Logos) of God. However, Logos christology need not be docetic. "That God has a 'Logos...,'" says Karl Rahner, simply means God is "historically faithful,"[41] that is, God communicates. And Cooke, again, makes it very clear that Logos christology need not result in idolatrous conflating of God and Jesus: "Jesus really functioned in his personal being, in everything he humanly was, as a word of the divine....[However] I would wish to preserve for the notion of 'word' ...a strictly functional implication."[42] To put this in our context, Jesus is a word about the divine in that his reverence, gratefulness, joy, silence, courage, creativity, justice, forgiveness, and compassion function to point to and draw some to God. And for Christians, he is the supreme word.

What slows the progress of Jews and Christians achieving deeper spiritual encounter as both incarnational people is the triumphal doctrine of Christ that develops in the centuries following the establishment of the Christian movement. Elizabeth Johnson paints a bracing picture of this unfortunate pattern:

> Historically as the early Church became inculturated in the Greco-Roman world, it gradually shaped itself according to the model of the patriarchal household and then to the model of Empire…Christ was then viewed as the principal of headship and cosmic order, the ruling king of glory, the Pantocrator par excellence, whose heavenly reign sets up and sustains the earthly rule of the head of the family, empire and Church.[43]

When we clear away the obfuscations of metaphysical christologies, as well as the brutalities to which their triumphalism has so often led, we Jews and Christian, and others, may experience together the humanistic richness of incarnation, how it points to human and divine locked in intimate embrace. Incarnation means that the human person, as Rahner says, is the "transcendental subject" who is in thrall to "what is boundless…nameless…absolute mystery." We see that it is the human person who is "the mystery," "[a] conscious orientation to this fullness," which is God.[44] Then incarnation is not a stumbling block between Jews and Christians, or members of any pair of humanistic religious communities. It is rather a deep and rich foundation for living out our spiritual vocations and revering one another.

The Moral Life

At its best, biblical, historical, and continuing contemporary Judaism embodies and promotes a vision and practice of moral life imbued with realism, emergence, humanism, communality, concreteness, ritual embodiment, and passion for justice. And in important ways, the Catholic spirit (broadly synonymous with the liberal Christian theological consensus) is precisely to "re-Judaize" Christianity's vision and practice of moral life.

Realism replaces the apodictic spirit in morals, that is, the absolute, certain, invariant, and legalistic approach to moral education. In place of hierarchic dictation, there is emergent moral insight. Dualism is rejected in favor of fond embrace of all that is truly human. The common good, though founded on the sanctity of each individual, nevertheless trumps private desire. A priori ethical intellectual schema are set aside in favor of insight from experience of trying to live well. Moral life is linked to sacramental action. And the prophetic view of justice, rather than the Greco-Roman philosophical and legal view, is supreme.

Age in, age out, various expressions of Christianity, not least of all among them Catholicism, fall away from the moral practice catalogued in the previous paragraph and come to serve the parallel disvalues, (apodicticism, hierarchy, dualism, etc.). This is what Landon Gilkey, cited earlier in this chapter, has in mind in his discussion of Catholic moralism, "the decades even centuries of earnest moralism," to which Gerald Sloyan also refers in his wise study entitled *Catholic Morality Revisited*.[45]

Not withstanding the centuries of lapsing into moralism, it should not be surprising to find lodged in many Christian hearts a desire to get back to Jewish basics. For Jesus himself, Sloyan points out, "was...the author of a tradition in human behavior that featured the best in Jewish biblical and post-biblical morality."[46] That "there was...a distinctly Christian morality from the start," is true only "if by that is understood a Jewish morality featuring certain emphases."[47] Again we find a deep affinity, a ground for mutual appreciation, an impetus to spiritual companionship.

We had occasion to introduce the foundations of Jewish and Christian moral realism, without so naming them, in chapter two. Both moral traditions reject what Richard McBrien calls "classicism" in favor of "historical consciousness." The one "conceives the moral life as that which conforms to certain preexisting norms...." But in the approach imbued with historical consciousness, "the emphasis...is on the 'subject' as historical and social....It deals more with moral issues...in terms of the particulars of the historical moment."[48]

We saw further in chapter two how this historical consciousness gives rise to the Christian school of moral reflection called "proportionalism," an emphasis that takes account of human limitation and development and recommends against fixed absolutes, instead inviting the moral agent to "be faithful to the complex and changing circumstances of our lives, doing as much good as possible and as little harm as necessary."[49] We noted earlier that this proportionalist approach is indebted to the Jewish moral idea and practice *P'kuach Nefesh*, that is, in a finite and changing world, many "lesser evils" can be endured in order "to save a life."

The inspiration of Jewish moral realism is probably (no pun intended) at play in the strain of "propabalist" moral reflection which arises in the history of Catholicism as a feature of eighteenth-century casuistry. Casuistry is the "case method" of moral reflection and practice in which circumstances are taken to be of great account. The "probabalism" that emerged from the movement holds that in seeking to act morally, that is, to live well, "the probable opinion of any respected (because learned) theologians could safely be followed...by the Christian seeking moral guidance."[50]

Probabalism's reliance on good faith "calculation" of what is best to do or refrain from doing in a particular circumstance shares in the spirit of talmudic moral reasoning. This is also so of the reliance, in both instances, on the value of study and consulting the learned.

But it is in rejecting rigorism that Jewish moral realism impinges Christian life most positively and in which the affinity in the moral realm is most pronounced. Of this, Milton Steinberg writes: "Judaism does not expect perfection from man....In this respect Judaism is mellower...more realistic. It thinks too well of God to portray him as exacting impeccability from flesh and blood. He is too responsible to ask that man walk but never slip."[51] And in the same key, we read in the second-century catechetical classic of primitive Christianity, the *Didache* ("The Teaching of The Twelve Apostles"), "If you can bear the Lord's full yoke, you will be perfect. But, if you cannot, then do what you can."[52]

We have already had occasion to note Judaism's essential democracy, at least in comparison with most forms of Christianity. No one person speaks for the Jewish people. *Halackha*, (not "law," but rather "how to be and how to go," in other words, the "way"), emerges from the lives of the Jewish people in community listening to their own experience, to one another, and to the learned among them.

Thus, it has been in Catholicism through many centuries apart from what Sloyan calls the "innovation" of ultramontanism, an ideology of utter concentration of moral and religious authority in the office and person of the pope. This innovation gathers momentum from the nineteenth century on. Before this there is more credit given the *sensus fidelium*, the "sense of the faithful," and a view of religious and moral authority in which "spelling out what the law of the gospels required...[was]...the province of the theologians."[53]

We have already had occasion to note the essential humanism of Judaism at its most vibrant and healthy. The same feature characterizes the Christianity of the Catholic spirit (or the liberal Christian consensus). And it certainly pertains to the realm of moral reasoning and practice. Consider again, for example, Rosemary Haughton's idea that the Catholic enterprise is "loving everything on earth to the point where earth becomes heaven." Surely this is inspired by the broad Jewish tradition that stands behind a saying such as this from the sages "He who sees a legitimate pleasure and does not avail himself of it, is an ingrate against God who made it possible."[54]

Certainly Christianity in its myriad expressions, and Judaism sometimes and to a lesser degree, falls away from this rich moral humanism. Sloyan explains the source for Christians: "Jesus' demand that no one or nothing in this world be preferred to the rule of God was subtly transformed into a despising of this world as if it were by definition corrupt."[55]

We have already noted, with Richard McBrien, that one of the essential features of Catholicism is that "our way to God and God's way to us is...a communal way." We have already encountered the passion for communality in Judaism and discussed the importance of a creative Jewish separateness and, in chapter one, Reb Soloveitchick's insistence on maintaining the integrity of Jewish communal boundaries. The intensity with which the communal value is held is further revealed when we consider, as noted earlier, the teaching of the great prophet Isaiah about unjust acts by any member of the Jewish people, bringing the righteousness before God of the whole Jewish community into question.[56]

In this we encounter another profound affinity between a mainline Judaism and the kind of Christianity we have been considering: the shared passion for ethics of the common good and justice for all. So, in ancient Israel, we have the beautiful and classic expression of this corporate morality in Amos' "I hate, I despise your feasts. I take no delight in your solemn assemblies, but let justice roll down like waters and righteousness like an ever flowing stream" (Amos 5:21–24). And two millennia later, its Catholic companion in the stirring words of the 1971 Roman Synod of Bishops: "Actions on behalf of justice and participation in the transformation of the world appear to us as a constitutive dimension of the preaching of the Gospels."[57]

The affinities in the moral realm continue, as both traditions are seen to embrace an historical and concrete approach. Remember McBrien's description of historical consciousness: "It deals more with moral issues in the concrete...." In his discussion of a typical pattern of response to innocent human suffering, Steinberg dramatizes the parallel concreteness and historicity of Jewish sensibilities. He says that when "dealing with evil Judaism is true to character. It makes no effort to obtain conformity on points of theory but is crisp and clear on what it expects by way of behavior. It expects a man...to recognize [evil]...and fight it."[58]

This passion for the concrete need not, indeed should not, deflect Catholic moral thought from continuing along the lines of sophisticated philosphical reflection on moral life for which it is rightly renown. Still, Sloyan points to the shared inheritance and to where the priorities must lie when he writes: "Jesus was primarily a teacher of the way people ought to act, not the way they ought to believe. He was a Jew...."[59]

The ritual of any religion is subject to corruption, devolving into fustiness, rote, magic, or appeal for private salvation through worship. Even in those religious communities possessing a long history of relating ritual to moral life, sight can be lost of how rich a school of compassion is the worship of God. Here we encounter an added feature of affinity between Jews and Christians of the Catholic spirit or the liberal Christian consensus. It is that at their best both seamlessly weave together worship of God and animating passion for justice and compassion, most especially for the oppressed. Worship is for presence in praise and penitence to both the Holy One and to the cherished suffering subjects of God's creative love.

This interweaving of worship and moral life is nowhere in Judaism more dramatically portrayed than in the dramatic placement in the Passover Haggadah of the injunction to all Jews of all times not to wrong a stranger or a sojourner, for Jews were themselves once strangers and sojourners in Egypt and in the desert.[60] The Catholic parallel rests in a renewed sense of the social and moral as well as personal spiritual richness of eucharistic celebration. Of this, Philip Rosato writes: "The eucharist would seem magical to man if it were understood as the only bright light in an otherwise dark and godless world....Christ's presence in the hungry of the world (Mt 25:30) and his presence in the eucharist (1 Cor 12:23–26) must be seen as complementary."[61] And the Latin American theologian Juan Luis Segundo points to the same value, drolly saying something is amiss when the eucharist is celebrated precisely the same way the day before and the day after the revolution.[62]

Finally, it is in their shared passion for justice that Jews and Christians should find the most fruitful grounds, in the moral realm, for recognizing each other as siblings, for deeper spiritual encounter, for spiritual companionship.

The Old Testament scholar, Gerhard von Rad, wrote of biblical Judaism (and those who know know this continues to be a hallmark of Jewish life today): "There is absolutely no concept in the Old Testament with so central a significance for relationships of human life as that of sedeqah, justice and righteousness."[63] And the specific focus for justice in biblical, historical, and ongoing contemporary Judaism "is concern for the widow, the orphan, the poor and the sojourner in the land."[64] And so, time and time again, in injunctions such as this and the ones below, we encounter the really radical Jewish justice ethic, justice for the hurt, the marginal, the brutalized, "...the sojourners the fatherless, the widows who are within your house shall come to be fulfilled" (Deut 14:29). And "Give justice to the weak and the fatherless, maintain the right of the afflicted and the destitute, rescue the weak and the needy" (Ps 82:2–4).

An equivalent passion for justice is to be found in the New Testament. Sloyan notes that it is sometimes said "of Jesus ungenerously that he taught nothing new, nothing that is not in the tradition."[65] Sloyan rightly ascribes this assessment to the embittering legacy of centuries of polemical texts of the Christian scripture being used against Jews. But one can turn to Matthew's gospel to find two texts that fully display Jesus' moral genius. The first is chapter five, the Sermon on the Mount. The second is chapter twenty-five, the end times discourse. In the first, Jesus is remembered as speaking of the eight "happinesses," or beatitudes, among which is "Blessed are they that hunger and thirst for justice, for they shall be satisfied." And in the end times discourse, Jesus associates himself utterly with those who are hungry, naked, thirsty, sick, and imprisoned, and links salvation itself to acts of justice and compassion for these, "the least." It may be that there is nothing new in Jesus' teaching. But as Sloyan says "Jesus did more than assume and teach the prevailing morality of his Jewish people. He featured its noblest elements in a combination that can only be considered remarkable."[66]

Reverence emerges as we know and appreciate more deeply the good faith and nobility of the yearnings of the "other." We seek to grow in appreciation for our common inheritance, certainly Jews and Christians, but, as relations evolve, for members of any two religious communities discovering for their benefit the commonality or complimentarity of religions. Between Jews and Christians of the liberal theological consensus we see common patterns in construing our religious communities, the intimacy of the divine-human encounter and the nature of moral life. As we grow in knowledge, understanding and reverence, we find allies in spiritual life, spiritual companions, beyond as well as within our religious communities.

Thomas Merton, Exemplar

Earlier I said that when "we see and understand the [religious] convictions of the other as illuminating common religious experiences, then we recognize the other as a companion...." In this process there is genuine theological discourse. But at the point where we turn from theological and moral discourse to "profile…a witness embodying…spiritual genius," actually lived by someone in a religious community on a spiritual path different from our own, we have turned, or really descended more deeply, from theology to "depth theology."

I propose then to conclude this essay on how reverence emerges by offering an exemplar of faithfulness to the human vocation nurtured in the Catholic Church, embodying the Catholic spirit, to propose him as a rich companion for those in many religious communities, on many spiritual paths. The witness or exemplar is Thomas Merton, the remarkable spiritual teacher of the last century who managed, without hardly ever leaving his Trappist monastery, to exercise a remarkable influence on issues of war and peace, civil rights, Jewish-Christian relations, the renewal of the Catholic Church, and the opening to the West of Eastern spiritual riches during the mid-twentieth century.

Merton embraced the spiritual humanism of the incarnational perspective. He celebrated life as a partnership with God in glorious purposes on this earth, no doubt a "vale of tears," but not a testing ground for "sinners in the hands of an angry God." And like the heroes of the Catholic spirit before him, Merton also celebrated the related conviction of the intimacy of the divine-human engagement. On life as partnership with god, Merton writes: "Either you look at the universe as a very poor creation from which no one can make anything, or you look at your life and your own part in the universe as infinitely rich, full of inexhaustible interest, opening out into the infinite further possibilities for study and contemplation and interest and praise. Beyond all and in all is God."[67] And expressive of the divine-human engagement: "At the center of our being is a point or spark that belongs entirely to God, which is never at our disposal, from which God disposes our lives….This little point of nothingness and of absolute poverty is the pure glory of God in us."[68]

Thomas Merton was born on January 31, 1915 in France. His mother, Ruth, a Quaker from the United States, died in 1921 when Merton was six years old. His father, Owen, a painter and a New Zealander, died in 1931 when Thomas was sixteen. Merton's brother, John Paul, born in 1918, joined the Royal Canadian Air Force during World War II and perished in a crash in 1943. (Of John Paul, Merton wrote the moving poem, a stanza of which appears in the dedication of this book.)

Born in France, young Merton was briefly in New York, then back to France and England while his father still lived, and then, orphaned, sent by his maternal grandparents who lived in Douglaston, Long Island, to an English school and subsequently, for one year, to Clare College, Cambridge University. There he led a dissolute life of drinking and carousing and, as the term used to be, "got a girl in trouble," got her pregnant. His grandparents yanked him back to the United States, and he enrolled at Columbia University from which he received a bachelors degree in 1938 and a masters—both in literature—in 1939. In these years he flirted with the Communist party, and developed a lifelong passion for jazz and appreciation of the black culture flourishing in Harlem. The 1960s radical Eldridge Clever, in his autobiography *Soul On Ice*, said that no white person ever wrote so deeply or well of Harlem as Merton.

Of this period in Merton's life, Lawrence Cunningham writes that "His love for hanging out in bars with friends had obviously not been slaked, despite his unhappy experience in England. Photographs from this period show him nattily turned out in three-piece suits, acting very much the big man on campus"[69]

But Thomas Merton almost from his childhood appears to have been a person of profound spiritual yearning. Later in life, and often, he associates himself with Augustine's cry to the Holy One: "Our hearts were made for thee and they are restless till they rest in thee." Toward the end of his Columbia days, Merton started taking instructions and became a Catholic. He was deeply affected by Jacques Maritian's evocation of genuine Catholic humanism, by Etienne Gilson's retrieval of the medieval Catholic idea of God as "Being Itself" (or as Eckhart says, as Existence itself), and by Gerard Manley Hopkins' "fusion of deep love for beauty with an intense awareness of the presence of God in the world."[70]

After completing his masters degree, Merton went to western New York State and taught at Saint Bonaventure University. Attracted by Franciscan ideals of simplicity, passionate spirituality, and love and service of the poor, he sought admission to the Franciscan order but was turned down, likely after giving too full an account of his life to that point. In the Spring of 1941, Merton made an Easter retreat at the Trappist monastery of Our Lady of Gethsemani outside Louisville, Kentucky. He sought admission to this most austere and medieval order of the Catholic Church and entered into the life of a Trappist (or Cistercian) monk on December 10, 1941.

It was an austere life that Merton entered. Of it, Flavian Burn, Merton's student and later his abbot, wrote: "We rose at two in the morning and spent long hours in the choir. There was no central heating and we wore heavy clothing…it was hard for most people to come in and have no chance to speak. The food was not plentiful, but work was. Eating two pieces of bread and not quite coffee…and then going down and splitting logs in the Winter, that was pretty rough."[71]

In his twenty-seven years as a monk, Merton thrived, even as he wrestled with the demands of monastic life.[72] Burns, again, gives us a picture of Merton's pronounced comic, even hilarious, side:

I liked him enormously in the scholasticate[73]—everyone did— because, while he could be serious in his spiritual direction talks, he was full of humor and jokes, and always buoyant. Like the first time I recognized him in the monastery. It was after the bell had rung and all two hundred monks were filing through the cloister to the church. And there, coming down the middle of the cloister in the opposite direction, was this one man, making signs to everybody, explaining why he was going in the wrong direction….He was a master of visual commentary, like during the readings in the refectory (dining room) or during chapter talks. Just with the raising of his eyebrows or a facial expression at what was being said or proposed, he would bring down the house in laughter.[74]

During these twenty-seven years, Merton became enormously influential, though he did not leave Gethsemani for a protracted period of time until the very end of his life in 1968. The influence began with the publication, in 1948, of Merton's spiritual memoir, the story of his conversion, *The Seven Storey Mountain*, a classic he was ordered by his superiors to write. Lawrence Cunningham writes of it:

The Seven Storey Mountain was a book of pilgrimage and conversion....Christian readers enjoy a certain frisson in reading about the life of a person who turned from sin and evil to a life of graced conversion. The converted sinner (the worse the sin, the better) was a staple of the evangelical tent meeting, and the theme was equally popular in the penny press of Catholicism. Catholic popular piety produced copious amounts of such literature....What distinguished Merton's book from the lot was that it told a tale that was so thoroughly modern. Here was the story of hard-drinking, cigarette-smoking, jazz-loving, left-leaning, poetry-talking bi-lingual, New York intellectual with European roots who chucked it all for monastic life. The only thing missing was any specific details abut his sex life. The Trappist censors had enough problems with the picture of his rather bohemian life in the final version of the manuscript, and the romantic dalliances were blue-penciled out as lacking in edification.[75]

Over those twenty-seven years, Merton became the single most profound and important Catholic voice recalling the ancient practices of contemplation and meditation, about which we will have more to say in chapter five. He also emerged as the most profound and important Catholic voice urging Western Christians especially, but also others in the West, to appreciate and learn from the great spiritual riches of other religious traditions: Muslim mysticism (or Sufism), Hinduism, Judaism and, especially, Zen Buddhism and Taoism.

In addition, Merton played an important role inspiring young Christians to support the black civil rights movement. (Martin Luther King, Jr. was slated to go to the monastery at Gethsemani just before he was murdered.) He was even more influential in the anti-war movement of the 1960s before being silenced by his superiors, concerned at the decorum of a monk of the times writing tracts against government war making and Church reluctance to condemn nuclear weapons. (Typically, Merton partially skirted the ban by privately publishing and distributing his "Cold War Letters.")

Merton was also accounted a poet of some substance and his poem on the Holocaust was published in the first edition of the *Journal for the Protection of All Beings*, in which Lawrence Ferlinghetti, of City Lights Bookstore, published the Beat poets.

Finally, and this should not surprise us, Merton revered Judaism and Jewish people and carried on numerous correspondences with Jewish thinkers, most warmly and memorably with Rabbi Heschel, to whom he wrote of his "latent ambition to be a true Jew under my Catholic skin."[76] And Merton played an important role in repudiating an early draft of the Second Vatican Council's document dealing with Jewish-Christian relations, one which still spoke of a "mission to the Jews," and its replacement with the historic text we have today, *Nostra Aetate* ("In Our Times: The Church's Relations with the Non-Christian Religions," 1965).

For legions of people around the world, Merton is the great spiritual master. A journal, *The Merton Quarterly*; The International Thomas Merton Society, and the sustained and substantial publication and sale of his vast output of writing keep his influence vital and real thirty-seven years after his death. Of Merton, the fourteenth Dalai Lama wrote: "When he died I felt I had lost personally one of my best friends, and a man who was a contributor for harmony between different religions and for mental peace. So we lost one, it is very sad. I think if he remained a longer period, I think if he remained still today, he would be one of my comrades to do something for mental peace....When I think or feel something Christian, immediately his picture, his vision, his face comes to me. To the present day. Very nice."[77]

Only a cursory overview of the richness of "clues" from Merton and from his own lived spiritual genius about how to be faithful to the human vocation is possible here. In chapter two we noted his explanation of "spiritual life" as life, a life that is awake to itself, unified rather than scattered, life in which we school our hearts to desire what is good. Merton is especially eloquent and persistent, throughout his writings and over many decades, in raising up the cultivation of silence and the practice of compassion as defining work for the spiritually mature. And one of the master strokes of his thought is always to link cultivating silence, or as he sometimes so expressively labels it "inner solitude," to link this with the achievement of "true self" contrasted with "false self."

Of silence, Merton writes "the truest solitude is not something outside you, not an absence of men or of sound around you, it is an abyss opening to the center of your soul."[78] And of "self," he writes, "The only true joy on earth is to escape from the prison of our own false self and enter by love into union with the Life Who dwells and sings within the essence of every creature in the core of our own soul."[79] And that there can be no living out of our true self without the cultivation of silence, this inner solitude:

No man who seeks liberation and light in solitude, no man who seeks spiritual freedom can afford to yield passively to the appeals of a society of salesmen, advertisers and consumers....Keep your eyes clear and your ears quiet and your mind serene. Breathe God's air. Work, if you can, under His sky....But if you have to live in a city and work among machines and ride in the subways and eat in a place where the radio makes you deaf with spurious news and where the food destroys your life and the sentiments of those around you poison your heart with boredom, do not be impatient but accept it as the love of God and as a seed of solitude planted in your soul. If you are appalled by those things, you will keep your appetite for the healing silence of recollection. But meanwhile keep your sense of compassion for the men who have forgotten the concept of solitude.[80]

As we will consider at length in chapter five, cultivating inner solitude, cultivating silence, is for one's own well being and at the same time it is a discipline for overcoming self-absorption, self-pity, selfishness, and hardheartedness. It is a discipline of compassion. Of this, of this "desert" of compassion, Merton writes most beautifully in his journals:

What is my new desert? The name of it is compassion. There is no wilderness so terrible, so beautiful, so arid and so fruitful as the wilderness of compassion. It is the only desert that will truly flourish like the lily. It shall become a pool. It shall bud forth and blossom and rejoice with joy. It is in the desert of compassion that the thirsty land turns into springs of water, that the poor possess all things.[81]

One of the most renowned and accomplished of the young men and women on whom Thomas Merton had such a great influence in the period of the 1960s around issues of racial justice, war and peace, and true spiritual maturity, is the peace activist James Forest. Speaking twenty years after Merton's death, Forest captures what may be the trait that provides us with Merton's greatest witness, a singular contribution to anyone in any religious community on any spiritual path. "Over the years," Forest says, "as I've thought back on Merton, his life, his legacy, the very rationale behind his life, it's become clearer and clearer that he was a man of remarkable fearlessness about life...I think he helped many of us to become less afraid."[82]

So, Merton's message, for anyone, is really the same, if we agree with Forest's summary, as the most oft repeated message of the Bible: "Do not be afraid." Or, what comes to the same thing: live!

Notes

1. Gabriel Moran, *Religious Body: Design for a New Reformation* (New York: Crossroad Books Seabury Press, 1974), p. 188.

2. Ibid., p. 189.

3. Karl Rahner, *The Shape of the Church to Come* (New York: Crossroad Books, Seabury Press, 1974), p. 82.

4. John Cornwell, *Hitler's Pope: The Secret History of Pius XII* (New York: Viking Penguin Putnam, 1999), p. 149f. This is the notorious insistence of Vatican officials that the leadership of the Catholic Center Party in Germany, the only viable resistance to Nazi ascendancy in the government, disband the party as a quid pro quo between the Vatican and the National Socialists for a new—Nazi—government signing a treaty with the Vatican, the Reich Koncordat of 1933.

5. Kertzer, *Pope Against*, op. cit., p. 126.

6. "Lambs into Lions," *New Republic*, June 2001, p. 35. Review essay of *Constantine and the Bishops: The Politics of Intolerance*, by H. A. Drake.

7. James Carroll, *Toward a New Catholic Church* (New York: Houghton Mifflin, 2002), p. 61f.

8. Wills, *Papal Sins*, op.cit., p. 299ff.

9. Pope John XXIII, *Pacem in Terris* (Peace on Earth), in David J. O'Brien and Thomas A. Shannon (eds.), *Renewing the Earth: Catholic Documents on Peace, Justice and Liberation* (New York: Doubleday, 1977), p. 138.

10. J. Metz, *The Emergent Church: The Future of Christianity in a Postbourgeois World* (New York: Crossroad, 1981), p.138.

11. James Carroll, "Redefining the Bad Catholic," *The Boston Globe*, November 22, 2003, p. A21.

12. Ibid.

13. Ibid.

14. Ibid.

15. Langdon Gilkey, *Catholicism*, op.cit., p. 18.

16. Ibid., p. 18f.

17. Milton Steinberg, *Basic Judaism* (New York: Harcourt Brace, 1975), p.71.

18. Ibid., p. 44.

19. Jacob Neusner, *The Way of Torah: An Introduction to Judaism* (Belmont, MA: Dickinson Publication Company, 1970).

20. McBrien, op cit., p.9f.

21. Rosemary Haughton, *The Catholic Thing* (Springfield, IL: Templegate, 1978), p. 234.

22. McBrien, op. cit., p.12f.

23. James Carroll, "Democracy in the Catholic Church," *Boston Globe*, May 14, 2002, p A15.

24. Moran, *Religious Body*, op.cit., p. 193.

25. Leo Baeck, *Judaism and Christianity* (Philadelphia: Jewish Publication Society, 1958), p. 135.

26. Elliot Wolfson, "Judaism and Incarnation" in Frymer-Kensky, Novak, etc., op. cit., p. 240.

27. Haight, op. cit., see chapter one, note 16.

28. Ibid., p. 200.

29. Ibid., p. 231.

30. Ibid., p. 238ff.

31. Ibid., p. 19.

32. Ibid., p. 200.

33. Ibid., p. 4.

34. Wolfson, op. cit., p. 240.

35. Ibid,. p. 243 and p. 244.

36. e.g. Gen 16:9–13; 18:2; 21:7; 22:11; Ex 3:2; 14:19; 23:21; 32:34; Jos 5:13; Jud 2:1; Isa 63:9; Ps 34:8.

37. Ibid., p. 247.

38. Ibid., p. 254.

39. Haight, op. cit., p. 178.

40. Bernard Cooke, *God's Beloved: Jesus' Experience of the Transcendent* (Philadelphia: Trinity Press International, 1992), p. 6.

41. Rahner, *Foundations*, op.cit., p. 215.

42. Cooke, op. cit., p. 9f.

43. Johnson, op. cit., p. 151.

44. Rahner, *Foundations*, op.cit., p. 216.

45. Gerald Sloyan, *Catholic Morality Revisited: Origins and Contemporary Challenges* (Mystic, CT: Twenty-Third Publications, 1990), p. 1.

46. Ibid., p. 16.

47. Ibid.

48. See chapter two, note 90.

49. See chapter two, note 91.

50. Sloyan, op. cit., p. 24.

51. Steinberg, op. cit., p. 89.

52. Cited in Sloyan, op. cit., p. 67f.

53. Ibid., p.24.

54. Steinberg. op. cit., p. 73.

55. Sloyan, op. cit., p. 16.

56. See chapter two, note 86.

57. Synod of Bishops, *Justice in the World* (Washington, USCC Publications Office, 1972), p. 34.

58. Steinberg, op. cit., p. 140.

59. Sloyan, p. 31.

60. Robert Goldstein (ed), *The Passover Haggadah* (Andover, MA: Temple Emanuel, 2003), p.22.

61. Noticed by this author when cited by David Hollenbach, SJ, in Philip Rosato, "World Hunger and Eucharistic Theology," *America*, vol 135, August 7, 1976, p. 48.

62. Juan Luis Segundo, *The Sacraments Today* (Maryknoll, NY: Orbis Press, 1974), p. 33.

63. Cited by John H. Donahue from Gerhard von Rad's *Old Testament*

Theology, in "Biblical Perspectives on Justice," in Haughey, op. cit., p. 68.

64. Ibid., Donahue himself, p. 73.

65. Sloyan, op. cit., p. 15.

66. Ibid.

67. Frontispiece of Montaldo and Hart, op. cit.

68. Quoted in Lawrence Cunningham, *Thomas Merton and the Monastic Vision* (Grand Rapids, MI: Eerdmans, 1999), p. 61.

69. Ibid., p. 7.

70. Ibid., p. 11.

71. Paul Wilkes, *Merton, By Those Who Knew Him Best* (San Francisco: Harper and Row, 1984), p. 105.

72. An especially fine treatment of Merton's struggles within monastic life and his continuing and ultimate affirmation of his life as a monk is contained in William Shannon's biography of Merton. *Silent Lamp: The Thomas Merton Story* (New York: Crossroad, 1992).

73. A scholastic is a student brother or monk; a scholasticate is a residence for scholastics.

74. Wilkes, op. cit., p. 107.

75. Cunningham, op. cit., p.33.

76. Ibid.

77. Wilkes, op. cit., p. 147f.

78. Thomas Merton, *New Seeds of Contemplation* (New York: New Directions, 1961), p. 57.

79. Ibid., p. 6.

80. Ibid., pp 84 and 87.

81. Montaldo and Hart, op. cit., p. 85.

82. Wilkes, op. cit.

CHAPTER FIVE

Praying Together

Thomas Merton says contemplation "is the highest expression of a man's intellectual and spiritual life. It is that life itself, fully awake, fully active, fully aware that it is alive. It is spiritual wonder. It is spontaneous awe at the sacredness of life, of being."[1]

The next stage, or perhaps the culminating stage in relations between Jews and Christians, or people in any two divergent religious communities whose relations are sufficiently evolved, is that we will sit together in contemplative or meditative prayer.[2] Every feature of the reconciliation of Jews and Christians, every stage, is rendered more vivid and effective set in the empowering context of engagement together in silent prayer. We will be silent together in God's presence. Such an experience in common overcomes theology's divisions and is, as I proposed earlier, effectively identical with what Heschel called "depth theology."

Contemplation takes dialogue beyond mere erudition and, at both personal and political levels if it is really contemplative prayer, it evokes the most profound compassion and hunger for justice. This precisely, in Merton's term, because it induces "spontaneous awe at the sacredness of life, of being." In other words, while contemplation is deeply personal, no human act is less individualistic, passive, or private. This is a point I will be at pains to emphasize throughout this chapter.

The capacity to engage in contemplation, to grow (in the words of the Buddha in the Dammapada "one by one, moment by moment, little by little"),[3] as a contemplative being is to cultivate the human mystical capacity. This human possibility should not be considered rare. The mystical capacity is the human ability to attend effectively to our inner lives, our "inner self."[4] Of prayer in general, Rabbi Heschel said that it is the act or practice "which saves the inner life from oblivion."[5] Is the inner life noisy and crazed or silent and peaceful? The question opens us immediately to the moral efficacy of contemplative practice expressing itself in personal charity and social justice. As Gabriel Moran writes:

> Mystics are accused of fleeing the world and not facing reality. But...the truth is that mystics not only "face reality" but embrace it....What is fled from is the trivializing attitude of grasping at goods that the human cannot carry beyond death, or demanding rights to the exclusion of other creatures. The moral and mystical journey is not to ideal and spiritual forms above the world but to the deepest, darkest center of the material cosmos where goodness bubbles up in gentle, just and caring attitudes.[6]

Contemplation Practice

Contemplative or meditative practice[7] is stopping, sitting comfortably, breathing deeply, calmly, and peacefully, returning consciousness and perception to the present moment in silence in order to more fully celebrate life's joys and bear with its sorrows, a practice that deepens our capacity to feel and to express gratitude and compassion. We know a great deal about how various meditative and yogic techniques induce a basic experience of calm and well being. In the United States, Herbert Bensen's *The Relaxation Response* and subsequently the work of Jon Kabit-Zinn occupy special, initiatory places in bringing the therapeutic or healing insights of ancient meditative techniques to the service of wholistic or "wellness" medical practice.[8] The work of the Project on the Contemplative Mind in Society advances these insights. In his 1996 work, *Emotional Intelligence*, Daniel Goleman seems to have stumbled onto the crucial relationship between contemplative practice and non-repressive control and channeling of emotional reaction, a link that is crucial to demonstrating the relation between moral practice and a meditative state of being.

Goleman rightly and richly identifies emotional intelligence with decentering the ego while not relegating or brutalizing the self, as in unhealthy asceticisms. He speaks regularly "of put[ing] aside one's self-centered focus," of "self-forgetfulness," and of a desirable "egoless" state.[9] However, he seems unaware that this loss of dominating ego without loss of self (what Merton speaks of as losing false self and gaining true self), is a principal purpose of contemplation and contemplative prayer. It is the point of Buddhist "sunyata" or emptying, and it lies beneath Saint Paul's evocation of Jesus Christ emptying himself ("kenosis") on the cross. It is what Rabbi Heschel means when he writes, "The self is not the hub but the spoke of a revolving wheel. In prayer we shift the center of living from self-consciousness to self-surrender....Prayer takes the mind out of the narrowness of self-interest and enables us to see the world in the mirror of the holy."[10]

Absent knowledge of, or at least reference to, contemplative traditions of practice, Goleman contrives such terms as "metacognition" and "flow" for what is in fact contemplation's role of inducing compassion, the ultimate concrete expression of the decentered ego.

Every school of practice of contemplation or meditation begins with stopping and attending to one's body. One assumes a posture conducive to achieving meditative aims. Slowly, patiently, one seeks, in the words of the Taoist sage, Chuang-Tzu, to "hold your being secure and quiet,"[11] by practicing a deep, calm, peaceful breathing pattern. In Jewish practice, this is linking one's own breath with "Nishmat Hayyim," "the breath of life" which emanates from God's own breath or spirit (*Ruah*). In this way, the devotee experiences *devekut* or "cleaving" intimately to the divine.

Not all contemplative or meditative practice is motivated by an intent to serve a transcendent moral practice. Many who meditate seek simply to induce in themselves calm and a heightened sense of well-being (and are more likely to call what they are doing meditation and not contemplation). Nevertheless, whenever genuine practice occurs, regardless of motive, something of great value is happening. For whatever the practitioner's intent, their companions and associates, and indeed the whole population of the world now and to come, all benefit however modestly when any human being, if only for a single moment, practices to be in harmony and to let go of fear and anger, or for that matter, lower back pain as well.

It is very important that the mundane purposes of contemplation or meditation practice not be disparaged in deference to more transcendental purposes, or the rootedness of all practice for whatever motive in attention to body be dismissed. For this technical, not complicated but technical, attention to the body—to breath pattern, to posture—is the indispensable ground for practice that deepens both personal peacefulness as well as deep gratefulness and compassion. My teacher, Gabriel Moran, knows this better than most. In his masterful study of responseability, we read, "The first step in being responsible is to listen to one's own bodily self. I realize this proposal might be construed as an endorsement of selfishness and narcissism. But these words describe individuals who do not realize that their self is split into speaker and listener. To know what the self really needs or wants, one must listen quietly and wait for deeper levels of the self to have their say."[12]

The next element of contemplative or meditative practice addressed is presence. We have already touched upon this quality.[13] Earlier, Rosensweig was cited equating the capacity to be present with revelation itself. Also noted was Everett Fox's translation of the name of God as intimately linked with the quality of presence. And Eudora Welty's haunting image of presence (and its absence) as the heart of human relations and of their demise was recalled.

In Christian tradition one of the great and profoundly simple texts with regard to presence is that associated with Brother Lawrence's *The Practice of the Presence of God*.[14] In Zen Buddhism, especially, practicing to be present is equated with nothing less than being free. The great Vietnamese spiritual teacher, Thich Nhat Hanh, gives us this very powerful teaching:

If you are still bound and haunted by the past, if you are still afraid of the future, if you are carried away by your projects, your fear, your anxiety and your anger, you are not a free person. You are not fully present in the here and now, so life is not really available to you. The tea, the other person, the blue sky, the flower are not available to you. In order to be really alive, in order to touch life deeply, you have to become a free person. Cultivating mindfulness can help you to be free. The energy of mindfulness is the energy of being present. Body and mind united. When you practice mindful breathing, mindful walking, you become free of the past, free of the future, free of your projects and you become totally alive again. Freedom is the basic condition for you to touch life, to touch the blue sky, the trees, the birds and the other person. This is why mindfulness practice [meditation] is very important....Train yourself to drink tea mindfully, to become a free person while drinking tea. Train yourself to be a free person while you make breakfast.[15]

This presence is not simply the premier therapeutic quality of consciousness, healing hauntings of the past, fear of the future, and the raggedness of being carried away by one's projects in the present. It is at one and the same time integral to moral living. Who, carried away by their projects as well as by fear, anxiety, and anger, can really respond effectively to others in either the personal or the political realms? Whether one acts well or badly in either realm is dependent on emotion. For emotion generates action: a kind word or a rebuke, just action to assist the disadvantaged or indifference masking embarassed privilege.

The whole of moral life, personal, interpersonal, and political, is dependent on how individuals and groups handle their emotions. Negative emotions are classically catalogued in the medieval Catholic seven deadly sins: lust, wrath, pride, envy, avarice, sloth, and gluttony. These find their counterparts in the overlapping roster of what in Buddhism are called the *Samyojana*, the nine "knots of forgetfulness of being": craving, rage, ignorance, pride, stubborn view, doubt, attachment, jealousy, and selfishness. Contemplative or meditative practice is the human capacity to "tutor ourselves," as Sidney Callahan writes, "within the constraints of the inner human program [to] voluntarily control, select, edit and engender emotional consciousness."[16] In *In Good Conscience, Reason and Emotion in Moral Decisions,* Callahan writes further that "emotions can be initiated and engendered at will from a state of rest or ground zero...the control strategy concentrates on using thought or inner speech to induce different emotional reactions. The key means of control is the human ability to freely deploy attention."[17]

Through free deployment of attention, once one gets good at its practice, we can replace anger with calm or envy with gratitude in the present moment. And at the deepest levels of contemplative or meditative practice, we can replace all speech—even the life-affirming inner counter-speech to fear, anxiety, and anger; even this can be replaced with silence.

The personal and therapeutic as well as the social and political importance of silence cannot be overstated, Merton's "inner solitude," Heschel's "treasures of silence." This is a state of presence filled with silence. No chatter, no inner voice of fear, anxiety or anger (and the aggression that follows), but silence. Typical of the importance attached to silence in all the great spiritual ways is this from Shaykh Fadhalla Haeri speaking of Sufism, Muslim mystical practice: "The spiritual masters share a state of inner silence and contentment. According to them, since the creation began from silence, anyone who wishes to start living must return to this point of origin—utter silence—an inner silence in which there is no vision, no memory, no thought, no movement."[18]

It is clear that the steady practice of the contemplative or meditative function assists practitioners to more readily "celebrate life's joys and bear with its sorrows." This practice composes the body, calms the breath, stills the shrill voice of "inner speech" preoccupied with the corrosives noted over and over again—chiefly fear, anxiety, and anger—and enables us to let go of past complaints and debilitating concern for the future while heightening awareness of gifts in our lives, the literal as well as metaphorical gifts to which Thich Nhat Hanh refers: tea, the blue sky, flowers, and the other person. The poet Rainer Marie Rilke expresses the link between contemplative silence and gratefulness: "Oh, if for once all were completely still. If all mere happenstance and chance were silenced, and laughter next door, too; if all that droning of my senses did not prevent my being wide awake then, with one thousand-fold thought, I would reach your horizon and for the span of a smile, hold you to give you away to all life as thanksgiving."[19]

So, there is much in contemplative or meditative practice for which to be personally grateful. But it is essential to fulfill the promise made earlier in this chapter by accounting for how contemplation feeds compassion. And the essential point to be made is this: contemplative practice nurtures greater expression of compassion precisely because it relativizes the ego in relationship to others. This is compassion's defining ingredient, this empathetic attentiveness to the other—suffering with the other—made possible by the ebbing of untoward ego.

Schopenhauer knew this; he called compassion "the primary and original phenomenon of ethics" and appreciated the link between compassion and the muting of self-absorption. He writes, "In that event [the practice of compassion] we abolish the partition that...absolutely separates one being from another; the non-ego has to a certain extent become the ego."[20]

To abolish the partition is to let go of the ignorant and illusory idea that we are, each atomic entity of us, utterly separate from one another and discrete, that we are absolutely distinguishable selves. To dispel this notion is an underlying goal of all the great religious communities and spiritual paths. One commentator writes of the theological anthropology of the early chapters of the Book of Genesis that the message is that human existence is "co-existence with others."[21] This powerful idea is dominant in both human creation narratives, those appearing in chapters two and three of the first book of the Hebrew Bible. In the former, both male and female are made in the one image of God; in the latter both come form the one flesh of the adama, the earth creature. In both instances, for all the varying uses to which the texts have been put over the centuries, the effect is to portray humans as part of one another. This is repeated often in classical Jewish spiritual sources, perhaps nowhere more profoundly then in the talmudic commentary on the children of Israel celebrating the destruction of Pharaoh's charioteers in the Red Sea. The commentary, positioned centrally in every year's Passover Seder, has God chiding his children, Israel, for celebrating what the Egyptians also "my children are drowning" (Megillah 10b).

The same sense of the common humanity of all persons, that we are intermingled, appears in the Advaita (non-dualism) school of Hindu spirituality. Here the devotee experiences the self (*jivatman*) as one with Atman, the great Self or Brahman. The essence of the experience is captured in the rapturous cry *Tat Tvm Asi*," "You are that!" And this is true of all: we are all one in Brahman.

The self same idea of human unity and the compassion it engenders is present in Jesus' reference, in the Gospel of Matthew, to all his followers as branches of the one vine and in Paul's elaborate and rich teaching on the "mystical body of Christ."

It is this same "reality of interdependence," as Thich Nhat Hanh designates it, that undergirds a defining Buddhist doctrine of the "Great Chain of Being." Through meditation, we experience that "the suffering of others is our own suffering and the happiness of others is our own happiness."[22]

Contemplative or meditative practice is, in significant measure, the process of getting rid of baggage, though in ways that are the polar opposite of self-help programs. In Sanskrit there is *upeksha*, letting go, *sunyata*, becoming empty, and *mokshe*, becoming free. "It is what we do not have—self-centeredness, immaturity, greed and anger—that enables us to live a compassionate life full of peace and freedom."[23]

Contemplation, Knowledge, and Interreligious Reverence

The symbols, rituals, beliefs, moral practices and patterns of common life in our religious communities necessarily bring us "knowledge": convictions about the meanings attached to what we believe and the effects of what we practice. This is as it must be, and throughout this book thus far I have proposed a variety of cautions so that our assertion of knowledge in the religious realm promotes movement together toward the Holy and not positivism, triumphalism, and, ultimately, brutality.

The spiritual master Abbot Thomas Keating writes, "The contemplative dimension of life, present in all the great religions, is the common heart of the world. There the human family is already one."[24] To acknowledge that beyond and below a conventional religious knowing, least of all a dogmatic positivism, the unspoken knowing of contemplation revealed in compassionate acts of peaceful persons, is the deepest common bond of people in different religious communities, this is already to lessen the brutality in the world. I need not rehearse here all previous caveats about the lethal effects of proud truth claims. But it is useful to say explicitly that siblings who sit in silent contemplation or meditation together know something in common, which is expressed not in formulas of "knowledge" but in a common pattern of gentleness and compassionate action. Gustavo Gutierrez calls this the one moment of simultaneous silences: the silence of contemplation and the silence of praxis, or transforming practice for justice and for peace.[25] The point is the same as that made earlier in contrasting David Novak's insistence on absolute truth claims with Abraham Heschel's intellectual humility. In recommending the priority of silence, the silence of contemplation and of praxis, Gutierrez says that theology should "only come out at night."[26]

Centering our interreligious engagement on contemplative prayer in common is the great antidote to arrogant assertions of exclusively true religious knowledge. In the words of the Taoist sage, Chuang-Tzu, "Not to know is profound; to know is shallow. Not to know is to be on the inside; to know is to be on the outside."[27] And from Sufi tradition: "The whole Sufi way of life is about giving up attachment and the worst attachment happens to be knowledge."[28] And finally, from the great Catholic theologian, Karl Rahner, "The act of accepting existence in trust and hope...is letting oneself sink trustfully into the incomprehensible mystery. Therefore, my Christianity...is...anything but an 'explanation' of the world and my existence."[29]

The God of Contemplative Prayer

Again, to fulfill the promise of relating contemplative or meditative practice to compassionate action, it is necessary to deal explicitly with the moral efficacy of a God encountered in this stillness.

Peter Berger identifies two modes of experiencing God: "confrontation with the divine," and "the interiority of the divine."[30] The distinction roughly parallels the experiences of God's transcendence and God's immanence and, again roughly and only partially, God as judge and God as consoling "near presence" (in Hebrew *Schekinah*). It is especially important to account for whether or not this God encountered in silent interiority carries sufficient moral heft or whether this is inevitably a God of "sentimental mysticism, self-help spiritualism, [a God] of Star Wars bliss seeking."[31]

Abraham Heschel, like Leo Baeck before him,[32] gives powerful—and droll—testimony to what he takes to be a God domesticated. Criticizing Paul Tillich, though in this context not by name, Heschel said in 1972:

> One of the most popular definitions of God in America today was developed by a great Protestant theologian: God is the ground of being. So everybody is ready to accept it. Why not? Ground of being causes me no harm, and I'm ready to accept it. It's meaningless. Isn't there a God who is above the ground? Maybe God is the source of qualms and of disturbing my conscience. Maybe God is a God of demands. Yes, this is God, not the ground of being.[33]

A parallel to Heschel's critique of what he takes to be a God domesticated is found in H. Richard Niebuhr's famous dismantling of the excesses of liberal Christianity run amuck. Niebuhr writes that for such liberals "A God without wrath, brought men without sin into a kingdom with judgment through the ministrations of a Christ without a cross."[34]

In the face of these warnings, how to answer the question whether the God encountered in contemplative stillness is sufficient to prod women and men to work for justice and to act with compassion? The answer is simple. If the God encountered in contemplative or meditative practice legitimates narcissism and passivity, this is not God and the process is not contemplative prayer. Consider again Merton's words, quoted in the previous chapter, that "at the center of our being is a point or spark that belongs entirely to God, which is not at our disposal, from which God disposes our lives...."[35] True contemplative or meditative prayer is the journey to the center and the experience of Divine presence as presence itself. But, to repeat Carol Ochs' wise words "Presence both heals and wounds, brings peace and unease, both satisfies and arouses desires..."[36]

The journey within is no escape from moral responsibility; it is integral to knowing the God who requires justice and compassion. And, as

Ochs again says, "When we know God only then will we know the self."[37] Contemplative prayer unmasks "false self," and assist us to let go of its toxins, "knots," "deadly sins." Thus emptied, our bodies and minds (our hearts really) become available for the works of justice and of peace.

Conclusion

Contemplation is often given expression in acts of charity that, of themselves, leave the structures of public policy untouched and therefore do not constitute acts of social justice properly so called.[38] The treatment of the relationship between compassion and contemplation is not complete without also addressing this point.

There is no guarantee that any given practitioner of contemplative or meditative prayer will carry the fruits of practice into the public policy realm. This is, of course, a specific stipulation that cannot be forecast. It is different from saying that where there is genuine contemplation there will follow inevitably acts of compassion. There are, nevertheless, hints that where contemplative practice is tied to moral energy finding expression in efforts to transform structures of economic and social life, the linkage is potent. Robert Thurman, the distinguished scholar of Tibetan Buddhism, implies how this works. He highlights how the contemplative virtues naturally conflict with disordered social structures. "Commercial interests, with their advertising industry, do not want people to develop contentment and less greed. Military interests in economic, political, ethnic or nationalist guise, do not want people to develop more tolerance, non-violence and compassion. And ruling groups, in general, in whatever sort of hierarchy, do not want the ruled to become too insightful, too independent, too creative on their own."[39]

And Jim Douglas, the evangelical social activist, makes explicit the relationship between fighting for social justice and sustaining oneself in such work through contemplative prayer. In his book *Contemplation and Resistance*, Douglas writes:

If resistance is the yang of liberation, contemplation is the yin....If we wish to pass into the living truth of Jesus or Gandhi, we must affirm, as they did, the way of liberation as neither the yang of resistance nor the yin of contemplation but rather the one indivisible way....As resistance seeks to liberate men and women from the pain of social injustice, contemplation seeks to liberate us from the pain of a yet deeper alienation: the impoverished and autonomous self.[40]

To return to Merton, how can a practice which induces "spontaneous awe at the sacredness of life, of being," fail to nurture a hunger for justice, and, doing so, unite people in different religious communities and spiritual paths in both compassion and contemplation?

Notes

1. Merton, *New Seeds*, op.cit., p. 1.
2. There is a difference in usage, over centuries, between the practice called "contemplation" and that called "meditation." There is also a convention, employed here, of using the terms interchangeably. In the case of both words, they are employed to designate a practice which is one of prayer and not a supposed only natural exercise which does not engage the divine-human relationship.
3. The complete text, adapted, from chapter XVIII, is "As a smith removes impurity from silver, even so, let a wise man remove impurities from himself, one by one, little by little, moment by moment." Quoted in Barnhart and Wong, op. cit., p. 126.
4. See Thomas Merton's exceptional study *The Inner Experience: Notes on Contemplation*, edited and introduced by William H. Shannon (San Francisco: HarperSanFrancisco, 2003).
5. See chapter one, note 14.
6. Gabriel Moran, *No Ladder to the Sky: Education and Morality* (San Francisco: Harper and Row, 1987), p. 3f.
7. See note 2 above.
8. See Herbert Benson, *The Relaxation Response* (New York: Avon Books, 1975). And Jon Kabit-Zinn, *Full Catastrophe Living: How to Cope With Stress, Pain and Illness Using Mindfulness Meditation* (New York: Dell Publishing, 1991).
9. Daniel Goleman, *Emotional Intelligence* (New York: Bantam Books, 1995), p. 46, 91f.

10. Dresner, op. cit., p. 20.

11. Thomas Merton, *The Way of Chuang-Tzu* (New York: New Directions, 1965), p. 128. Merton rendition of the sage's story "Keng's Disciple."

12. Gabriel Moran, *A Grammar of Responsibility* (New York: Crossroad, 1996), p. 86.

13. In the discussion of revelation in chapter 3.

14. Brother Lawrence, *The Practice of the Presence of God* (Springdale, PA: Whitaker House, 1982). Brother Lawrence lived in the seventeenth century.

15. Thich Nhat Hanh, *Anger: Wisdom For Cooling the Flames* (New York: Riverhead Books, 2001), p. 44f.

16. Sidney Callahan, *In Good Conscience: Reason and Emotion in Moral Decision Making* (San Francisco: Harper and Row, 1991), p. 112. Callahan does not refer explicitly in this section of her book to contemplative practice. I have drawn the implication.

17. Ibid.

18. Shaykh Fadhlalla Haeri, *The Elements of Sufism* (New York Muslim Books, 1991).

19. Cited in Brother David Steindl-Rast, *Gratefulness, the Heart of Prayer: An Approach to Life in Fullness* (New York: Paulist Press, 1984), p. 30.

20. Schopenhauer in Wolfgang Schirmacher (ed.), *Philosophical Writings* (New York: Continuum Publishing, 1996) p. 204.

21. Cited by McBrien in discussing biblical anthropology, op. cit., p. 126.

22. Thich Nhat Hanh, *Being Peace* (Berkeley, CA: Parallax Press, 1987), p. 48.

23. Sunyana Graef, "A Hair in Vast Space: Teaching and Learning in Zen," *Religious Education,* vol 84 #2, (Sp 1989, p. 181).

24. Thomas Keating, OCSO, *The Heart of the World: A Spiritual Catechism* (New York: Crossroads Press, 1981), p. 1.

25. Gustavo Gutierrez, *On Job: God-Talk and the Suffering of the Innocent* (Maryknoll, NY: Orbis Press, 1987), p. xiii.

26. In personal conversation, but also implied in the citation above, number 25, where Gutierrez says first there is the two-pronged moment of silence, the silence of contemplation and of practice, and only after that may there be speech.

27. Cited in Barnhart and Wong, op.cit., p. 211.

28. Shaykh Fadhalla Haeri, op. cit., p. 38.

29. Karl Rahner, *The Practice of Faith: Handbook of Contemporary Spirituality* (New York: Crossroad, 1983), p. 7.

30. Peter Berger, *The Heretical Imperative: Contemporary Possibilities of Religious Afformation* (New York: Crossroad, 1979), p. 168.

31. Tom Appelo, "God Still Ready for His Close-Up," *New York Times*, May 11, 2003, p. 29.

32. In *The Essence of Judaism*, Baeck criticized "romantic religion," which he considers Christianity to be a principal example of, as focusing on feeling, prone to sentimentality, and insufficiently ethically responsible (New York: Schocken Books, 1961), p. 70.

33. S. Heschel, op. cit., p. 246.

34. H. Richard Niebuhr, *Christ and Culture* (New York: Harper Torchbooks, 1961), p. 104.

35. Merton, *Conjectures of a Guilty Bystander*, in Cunningham, *Merton*, op. cit., p. 61.

36. Carol Ochs, *Song of the Self*, op. cit., p. 98.

37. Ibid., p. 101.

38. Catholic Social Teaching, capitalized as a proper nominal designation of a recognized body of evangelically inspired but philosophically and ethically sophisticated teaching dating to Pope Leo XIII in 1879, carries illuminating distinctions between charity and justice and among several forms of justice. See chapter four, note 9.

39. Robert. Thurman, "Meditation and Education: Buddhism, India, Tibet and Modern America." A monograph of the Project on Contemplation in Society, 1996, p. 2.

40. James Douglas, *Resistance and Contemplation: The Way of Liberation* (New York: Doubleday and Company, 1972), p. 53.

Education For Reverence

I conclude this work with some further thoughts on education, thoughts that supplement the discussion of religious education in chapter two and provides a further context for the discussion of contemplation education just concluded.

The Breadth of Education and Its Usefulness

Education is the sum of relations in which we engage for the purpose of nurturing one another to live well and in genuine happiness. Education is nothing less than helping one another practice faithfulness to the human vocation, which is to work on our masterpiece, ourselves, what Rabbi Heschel calls our "work of art." A human work of art grows, over the course of a lifetime, more reverent, grateful, joyful, still, creative, courageous, just, forgiving, and compassionate. In a life lived in conscious interchange with the divine, practicing faithfulness, finally, includes praise and penitence before the Holy One. Education is practice which is always intentional but not always conscious.

I had occasion in chapter two to note Gabriel Moran's more—than typically—expansive view of education as relational practice that transcends one social form, school, and occurs, or is thwarted, in other influential social forms of human living: family, recreation, and job. The insight about there being a multiplicity of social forms in which educating occurs provides us with insight about the many venues in which interreligious reverence can grow, whether between Jews and Christians or other pairings. This is not a small thing. "To study in the presence of the other," is one of the rich foundational principles of The Catholic Jewish Colloquium, which we first encountered in chapter two and which we will consider here again. The same principle can be applied across all the social forms of education and provide an explicit programmatic agenda for religious educators who seek to serve both functions of such practice: nurturing the members of the religious community in loyalty to its path of spirituality and also in reverence for our siblings—also God's children—in other religious communities.

Moran's equally instructive appreciation of the diversity of the act of teaching (as he says "to show how") is also suggestive for this work. Teaching by example invites us to remember to point out the saints not only in our midst but in their midst as well. Teaching by design Moran associates especially, though not exclusively, with coaching. And certainly members of religious communities can be coached to understand differently who they are in relationship to the "others."

Moran's third mode of teaching is teaching with an end in view, exposing people to rhetorical influence in story, lecture, and sermon. This is a necessary strategy for making a compelling case for interreligious reverence. Moran identifies teaching to remove obstacles with employing therapeutic language that calms, soothes, heals, and praises, language that comes into play when acrimony has soured relations and rendered reverence remote.

Finally, there is teaching the conversation, speaking (and listening) so that greater understanding becomes possible.[1] And here we return to the model of The Catholic Jewish Colloquium of 1993-95.

The Catholic Jewish Colloquium

The fullest accounting of this model 1993-95 experiment in education for reverence appeared in the Fall, 1996 issue of the journal then called *Religious Education*, in an essay entitled "The Catholic Jewish Colloquium," authored by Mary C. Boys and Sara Lee.[2] There are four remarkable features of this educational experiment, the fourth and perhaps the most meaningful playing into and underscoring a principle thesis of this book: that finally members of different religious communities, on different spiritual paths, must find ways to pray together to acquit the deepest hopes for interreligious relations. The four features to which I have reference are 1. the expertise in educational practice characterizing the Colloquium; 2. the fact that the members of the two religious communities studied in one another's presence; 3. the mutuality of expectations which motivated the study; 4. that the participants discovered the yearning to pray together.

The Colloquium met six times for two-day sessions each time over the period of three years. More impressive than the sheer time spent is the depth and range of what was studied and the human and material resources brought to bear. The first colloquium meeting dealt with "The Asymmetrical Character of Judaism and Christianity," the second with "Jews and Christians in the First Two Centuries," the third "Revisiting the History in the Presence of the Other," the fourth "Judaism and Catholicism in the North American Context," the fifth "The Educational Task of Catholic-Jewish Dialogue" and the final session "Religious Education and the Work of Interreligious Learning."[3] In addition to Boys and Lee, scholars and teachers of enormous gifts, many other gifted resource persons interacted with the leaders in Jewish and Catholic religious education who participated in the Colloquium.

The second feature of the colloquium is self-evidently central to the "interreligious learning": which was its goal: the study was done together. But, the third feature of the Colloquium is equally important. Though one may question the extent of mutuality of learning as I did in chapter two, at least until one reads of the touching desire to know one another deeply that participants expressed, still a stated purpose of the Colloquium was for Catholics "to rethink their identity and vocation through a sustained encounter with Judaism and Jews," and for Jews "an opportunity to learn about Christianity from the inside," an opportunity the leaders of the Colloquium felt necessary for Jewish participants to "liberate themselves from a view of Christianity as primarily predicated on the rejection and persecution of Jews."[4]

Boys and Lee tell us that "after session one the participants indicated a strong desire to 'get inside' the other's tradition of faith...[to] transcend the rational and to give the others a 'feel' for the soul of Catholicism and Judaism through sharing of practices."[5] They tell us further that a response to this was the framing of a blessing before meals taken from Psalm 19:4: "May the words of my mouth, and the meditations of my heart, be acceptable to you O Lord, my rock and redeemer." And in a deeply moving report about the end of the three-year colloquium, an ending marked by shared worship, by celebrating together a Service of Praise and Thanksgiving, participant Shulamith Reich Elster writes

> We began: "We Jews and Christians want to uplift our words. We desire to free our words of meanings that hurt each other, to wash away the words that have for so long separated us and set us against each other. We long for a renewed language, for words that powerfully convey our need to be together, our desire to honor and esteem each other's faith.... "[6]

I have no doubt that the caring and gifted people who framed, conducted, and participated in this remarkable experiment know the truth of Thomas Merton's words: "The highest form of religious worship finds its issue and fulfillment in contemplative awakening and in transcendent spiritual peace—in the quasi-experiential union of its members with God, beyond sense and beyond ecstasy."[7]

The fullness of engaging one another as siblings, as all God's children, the fullness of spiritual companionship, awaits lifting up not only our words but also our silence. No one knows themselves sufficiently if they do not encounter the Holy One. And we cannot know one another adequately, as spiritual companions, until we too, Jews and Christians or members of any two religious communities, experience God's silence together. It is for this reason I conclude with a prayer of brother John Hammond, OSB, and of the Benedictine brothers of Weston Priory:

> Companions, the wise tell us that God abides in silence, that God abides in the silence of the heart. Let us not speak of silence, rather let silence speak to us of God. Together let us enter through the door of serenity the silence of our hearts. The chatter of our fears, our angers, our anxieties, the chatter of our desire and curiosity, of our projected plans and unfinished work fall away in serenity and makes space, an open space for a new heart, created in the silence of prayer, created in the prayer of silence. A heart that is free, peaceful, quiet and calm, a heart that is one, a heart so large and wide that it embraces the God of all and the all of God. The God who in silence speaks in all creatures, the God who in silence speaks in all languages, the God who in silence speaks one word, the God who speaks of love.[8]

Let us raise up contemplation education as the next great moment and practice for reverence between spiritual companions.

Endnotes

1. Gabriel Moran, *Showing How: The Act of Teaching* (Valley Forge, PA: Trinity Press International, 1997).
2. Volume 91, #4. Most of this volume of the journal was devoted to reporting on the colloquium.
3. Ibid., p. 430–432.
4. Ibid., p 423f.
5. Ibid., p. 432f.
6. Ibid., p. 574.
7. Merton, *Inner Experience*, op. cit., p. 26.
8. Brother John Hammond, OSB. Portion of an untitled prayer contained on the CD of the monks of Weston Priory entitled "Hear the Song of Your People." Produced by the Benedictine Foundation of the State of Vermont, 1998.

Acknowledgments

There is, first of all, a great army of women and men known to me who edify me by their practice of living well. Because their goodness transcends borders of religious community and spiritual paths while rooted therein, for that very reason they teach me over and over the truth of a radical religious pluralism, the aptness of interreligious reverence. That is to say, their goodness, and the good they do, is without reference to any special claims to God's only or principal affection. They are too numerous to name. So, apart from two who must be named, my beloved wife and son, Margaret (Peggy) O'Hare and Brian ("Bucky") O'Hare, I rest in the hope and confidence that though unnamed they know what they mean for me, especially since, in truth, I do not neglect to tell them so from time to time but regularly.

Thanks to Gwen Costello for finding in this manuscript a book that might be read with benefit, and to Mary Carol Kendzia for expert editing and collaboration. And thanks to Pat and Neil Kluepfel, founders of Twenty-Third Publications, for a million laughs and more inspiration, chiefly that the Church of Papa Roncalli might survive and prosper. And, too, for a night of lobsters, a baby boy, and a puppy.

There are those who lent specific and invaluable help in specific ways, and for them I am grateful. Dick Tresch, of the economics faculty of Boston College, for pressing me on the matter of truth claims. Harvey Egan, SJ, of the theology faculty of Boston College, for help interpreting the great Rahner. And Larry Lowenthal, of the American Jewish Committee in New England, for specific insight and bibliographic advice about the value of Jewish separateness.

Two of the great friends who read this text, in manuscript, with such generosity and appreciation that their enthusiasm bolstered me while I "peddled" it should be mentioned here. These are William ("Doc") Miller of Facing History and Ourselves and Michael St. Clair of Emmanuel College. In this same category, as friend and one who nur-

145

tures hope through generous praise, I number, as well, Joseph Kelley, provost of Merrimack College, and colleagues on the faculty of religious and theological studies. Like the final four—people and groups—mentioned below, Kelley, Miller, and St. Clair lent inspiration and confirmation. For this contribution and for their friendship I am deeply grateful.

Well over thirty years ago, my teacher (and friend) Gabriel Moran opened for me a world where it might be possible to be thoroughly rooted in a religious community and yet not believe that this community alone is God's only people. This teaching results from his continuing and uniquely inspiring insight about the reality of revelation. If anything, his historical wisdom about the depth, richness and mutivalency of the relational exchanges people call "education," has been and remains even more defining of my life's intellectual contours and personal passions. His wife, Maria Harris, also my teacher and friend, who died on the feast of Brigit of Kildare, February 1, 2005, may, if it is possible, be even more influential on what I've come to believe is true and to be done in the professional realm. For she led me, or more precisely I followed her, from one adventure to another, during especially formative young adult years, this to my undying benefit.

James Carroll is for me the principal public intellectual today handling theological ideas. A public intellectual is one who is especially attentive to and effective in vividly representing ideas to the public in ways that draw lines compellingly between these ideas and public policy. He is a dear friend and unflagging in courage to speak about how deep the incision into Church triumphalism must cut to excise religiously inspired xenophobia and thereby save both the "other" and the triumphalist.

Until my friend, Bob Bullock, died and thereby changed the plan for dedicating this book, my plan, of several years, was to dedicate it to one individual and to one group of men.

At a day-long workshop on Christian Preaching and Interreligious Relations held in 2002 at Merrimack College, sponsored by its Center for the Study of Jewish Christian Relations, Bob Bullock sought to characterize the breadth and depth of what is owed Bishop Krister Stendahl. Bullock was addressing thirty-five or forty Orthodox, Catholic, and Protestant priests and ministers who cared enough about interreligious reverence to come for a day to study how to preach well of Christ Jesus without, in Stendahl's wonderfully droll appraisal, "telling bad stories about others." After ticking off a string of qualities and accomplishments, Bob threw up his hands as if to say that nothing quite encompasses all we owe Bishop Stendahl and then said simply, "He's our Michael Jordan." Priest, bishop, scholar, teacher, friend, above all mentor to so many and so richly, I join a legion of women and men who care about these matters whose debt to Krister Stendahl cannot be paid.

There are finally to be thanked the Benedictine monks of Weston Priory in Vermont. They provide for me and my family, and for a great many, a spiritual home, a model of life lived graciously and well (a simple life, but not easy). Not coincidentally, this authentic monastic community, this oasis, was established by a man on fire with a dream of contemplative practice and non-violence, a dream of interreligious love and spiritual companionship across lines of religious difference, especially between Jews and Christians. This was Abbot Leo Rudloff.

Thomas Merton may have been writing of the monks of Weston Priory:

> The monastic flight from the world into the desert is not a mere refusal to know anything about the world, but a total rejection of all standards of judgment which imply attachment to a history of delusion, egoism and sin. Not of course a vain denial that the monk too is a sinner (this would be an even worse delusion), but a definitive refusal to participate in those activities which have no other fruit than to prolong the reign of untruth, greed, cruelty, and arrogance in the world of men. The monastic withdrawal from secular time is then not a retreat into an abstract eternity but a leap from the cyclic recurrence of inexorable evil into the escatological kingdom of God, of Christ—the kingdom of humility and of forgiveness. (*Seeds of Destruction*)

Amidst all the contributions that these brothers make, by their teaching and by their example, to building up the authentic humanity and hunger for justice of those fortunate enough to share a measure of their life and practice, it may be sufficient here to report this: when Christians leave Good Friday prayer with the brothers each year, they go out celebrating with gratitude the gift of their Jewishness.

Index

Accounting For Fundamentalism, by
  R. Scott Appleby and Martin Marty,
  12
Action christology, 65
Aquinas, Thomas
  mystery of God, 84
  and revelation, 92
Ad Gentes, on interreligious reverence,
  14
Advaita Hinduism, 133
Amos, the Prophet, 113
Anselm, Saint, on theology, 9
Anti-Judaism, 28
Antisemitism, 28
Apetheia, 2
Apophatic way, 5
Aristotle on friendship, 79
Atman, 2
Augustine of Hippo, Saint
  on interiority, 6
  and the mystery of God, 84
  and revelation, 92
Auschwitz, 33

Baeck, Leo on Jesus, 105
Baum, Gregory on critical theology, 77
Bauman, Paul on James Carroll, 41, 81
Benson, Herbert, 127
Berger, Peter on experiencing God, 134
Boys, Mary C. 8ff, 54, 142ff
  Catholic-Jewish Colloquium, 9,
  142ff
  on anti-Judaism in the Letter to the
  Hebrews, 20
  Tradition and transformation, 54
Buber, Martin, receiving revelation, 85
Burn, OCSO, Flavian on Thomas
  Merton, 118
Buddhism Zen, 5f, 133
  Vatican official on, 13f
  Mahayanna, 14
  and the Bodisattva, 14

Callahan, Sidney on emotions, 130f
Cantwell Smith, *Catechism of the
  Catholic Church*, 33
  on baptism, 38
Catholic-Jewish Colloquium, 8ff, 55,
  141ff
Catholic Morality Revisited, by
  Gerald Sloyan, 110
Catholic Social Teaching, 139
The Catholic Thing, by Rosemary
  Haughton, 112
Carroll, James, 81
  Contradictions in Pope John's Paul
  pontificate, 38
  Genuinenss of Catholic Church
  response to Jewish people, 40
  Criticized in *Commonweal*, 41
  Krister Stendahl's assessment of
  Constantine's Sword, 77
  and Jesus' rejection of Roman
  imperium, 101
  and "good" and "bad" Catholics
  102f
Chaung-Tzu on knowing and not
  knowing, 134
Christ in Jewish Terms, Tikva
  Frrymer-Kensky, David Novak, (ed)
  et al., 7
Christ of conciliar renewal, 35f
Christology and docetism, 18
  the liberal Christian theological
  perspective, 65f, 105-109
  and triumphalism and Jewish-
  Christian spiritual companionship,
  109
  existential, 65, 107
  and Christ as king, 109
Church in liberal Christian theological perspective, 64f
  as power structure, 100
  rigorous instead of radical, 102
  treatment of sexuality, 103

Classicism as method in moral reflection, 66
Cleaver, Eldridge on Thomas Merton, 117
Cobb, John, 11ff, 22ff
Coe, George Albert on religious education, 53
Coles, Robert on saints in our midst, 59
Coming Convergence of World Religions, The, by Robley Whitson, 40
Compassion and contemplation, 132ff
Conciliar reform and renewal, 35f
Conn, Walter, 10
Contemplation defined, 126
  and meditation, 137
Contemplation and Resistance, by James Douglas, 136f
Constantinian Catholic Church, 68, 101
Cook, Bernard on Jesus' Abba experience, 108
Cornwell, John author of Hitler's Pope, 101f
Cook, Francis on Vatican criticism of Buddhism, 14
Crossing the Threshold of Hope, by Pope John Paul II, 13
"Critical principle," (Rosemary Radford Ruether), 78
Cunningham, Lawrence on Thomas Merton, 177, 119
Cunningham, Philip anti-Judaism in the Letter to the Hebrews, 20
Cusa, Nicholas of, 78
Cyprian on the ideal of a bishop, 64

Dabru Emet (to speak the truth), 16, 50
Dalai Lama on Thomas Merton, 120
Dammapada of the Buddha, 137
de Leon, Moses, 20
Dershowitz, Alan on the vanishing American Jew, 47f
Devekut (cleaving to the Holy One), 127
Dialogue, 7

and beyond dialogue, 7, 51
and going beyond the "Age of Monologue," 79
"depth dialogue," 76
Didache (The Teachings of the Twelve Apostles), 111
Doctrinal development, 91
Dominus Iesus, 34, 37
Douglas, James, 136f
Dualism, 103, 110
  and twisting Jesus' moral teachings, 112
Dulles, SJ, Cardinal Avery and theological anti-Judaism, 19
  and three dimensions of faith, 87
  and revelation, 87
Dupuis, SJ, Jacques 24

Eckhart, Meister on God as Existence, 117
Education defined, 9, 140
Education for Religious Particularity and Pluralism Project, 55
Ellenson, David, 8f
Elster, Shulamith Reich, 143
Emotions and contemplation and compassion, 130f
Emotional Intelligence, by Daniel Goleman, 127
Enduring Covenant, The: The Education of Christians and the End of Antisemitism, by Padraic O'Hare, 59, 99
Eucharist and justice, 114
Evargrius on the theologian, 8
Existential, 23
  existential Christology, 65, 107

Faithfulness, 86
  to the human vocation, 23, 86
Ferlinghetti, Lawrence, 120
Fideism rejected in Catholic theological tradition, 91
Fox, Everett on the name of God in the Book of Exodus, 82
Forest, James on Thomas Merton, 122
Freedom and contemplation, 129

Fredrickson, Paula on Constantine
and the Church, 101
Friendship in Aristotle, 79
and reformed notions of revelation,
79
Fundamentalism, 12

Gelernter, David on separateness and
the Jewish people, 20ff
Gilkey, Langdon on Catholicism, 90f,
103, 110
Gilson, Etienne and Thomas Merton,
117
God as mystery, 84
immanence of in Irenaeus, 88f
immanence of in Gregory of Nyssa,
89
Goldhagen, Daniel, 14
Goleman, Daniel, 127f
Gregory of Nyssa on God's immanence, 89
Greenberg, Irving on God's love and
choosing, 24f, 54
Griffith, OSB, Bede, 2, 23
Groome, Thomas and dialectical
function of religious education, 89
Gutierrez, Gustavo on silence of contemplation and of praxis, 134

Haeri, Shayka Fadhalla on Sufism,
131
Halackha, 111
Hammon, OSB brother (small "b"),
144
Haight, SJ, Roger, 6
and creation and revelation, 83f
and Jesus as symbol of God, 106f
Hartman, David, 54
*Has God Only One Blessing?
Judaism as a Source of Christian
Self-Understanding*, by Mary C.
Boys, 10, 42
Haughton, Rosemary, 112
Havdala, 21
Heidegger, Martin, 50
and reception of revelation, 86
Hebrews, Letter to and anti-Jewish
interpretation, 19

Heschel, Abraham Joshua
meeting in humility, 7f
and prayer, 5
and searching together, 7, 38, 46
and the divine in a morsel of
bread, 18
and theology distinguished from
depth theology, 8, 47
and a man [sic] with no problems,
10
and revelation, 18
and a sense for the unique, 21
and the societal importance of religion, 32
and the limits of religion and
dogma, 41
and life as art, 44
and the critique of religion, 45
and Judaism as the mother of
Christianity, 46
accused of relativism, 46f, 72
and the "pre-theological" situation,
56
and encountering the personhood
of the other, 59
and God's universal presence, 81
and the mystery of God, 85
and Thomas Merton, 120
and the criticism of the idea of
God as "the Ground of Being," 135
Hicks, John and salvation, 21
and revelation manifest in practice, 93ff
Hillul Hashem, 31, 46
Hitler's Pope, by John Cornwell, 101
Holocaust, 15
"Holy Envy," 8
Holy Spirit, gifts of, 94
Hopkins, Gerard Manley, influence on
Thomas Merton, 117
Hubner, Dwayne on education, 9
Hyers, Conrad, on humor, 4

Incarnationalism, Jewish and
Christian, 105f
Eliot Wolfson on, 105ff
in thought of Karl Rahner, 109

Icons of the Present, by Edward
Robinson, 119
*In Good Conscience, Reason and
Emotion,* by Sidney Callahan, 130
International Thomas Merton Society,
120
Irenaeus on God's immanence, 88f
Issac, Jules, *Has Christianity Anti-
Semitic Roots?* and "teaching of
contempt," 14

Jesus of Nazareth, 2
Jesus, Symbol of God, by Roger
Haight, SJ
*Jewish-Christian Dialogue: A Jewish
Justification,* by David Novak
Jewish-Christian relations, stages of
development, 41ff
Jewish incarnationalism, 107f
Jewish moral realism, 111
Jivatman, 2, 133
John XXIII, Pope 31, 34, 37, 53
and suppressing the anti-Jewish
Good Friday prayer, 76

John Paul II, Pope, on Buddhism on
liberalism, 13
and the Covenant with the Jews, 16
and Jewish-Christian relations
restorationism in the Church, 33-38
and "classicist" foundation for his
moral thought, 66
John XXIII
on women in *Pacem in Terris,* 102
Johnson, CSJ, Elizabeth and the mystery of God, 84
and triumphal christology, 109
Jungmann, Joseph Andreas, 87
Justice, constitutive of faith, 113
and worship in Judaism and
Christianity, 113f
centrality in Jewish teaching, 115

Kabit-Zinn, Jon, 127
Kertzer, Robert, 15, 105
Keating, OCSO, Abbot Thomas on
contemplative dimension of religion, 133

Kenosis, 127
Kiddush Hashem, 31, 46
King, Jr, Martin Luther, 119
Klenicki, Leon on Jewish-Christian
relations and "triumphalism of
pain" and of "memory," 54
Knitter, Paul on John Cobb's views on
religion, 11f, 22f
on "unitive pluralism," 47
Kogan, Michael, 16, 60
Kolbe, Maximillian, 34

Language and religion, 17
Law, Cardinal Bernard on the ordination of women, 129
Lawrence, Brother, 129
Lee, Sara and the Catholic-Jewish
Colloquium, 8f, 54, 142f
Lefebure, Leo, 80
Liberal Protestantism in the United
States and Judaism, 63
and the Liberal Christian theological consensus, 64ff
Liberal theological perspective (view,
consensus, imagination), 12f, 61
and theological language, 17
perspective on Church, Christ and
moral life, 61-69
on Church, 100-105
on Christ, 105 - 109
on moral life, 109-115
Lonergan, Bernard, 10
on disclosure of the self through
others, 23

Macquarrie, John on the existential
dimension of Christology, 18
on calculative and primoridal thinking and revelation, 50
Maritain, Jacques, influence on
Thomas Merton, 117
McBrien, Richard P on classicism and
historical consciousness, 66, 110
on faith, belief and theology distinguished, 86f
on rationalism in the history of
Catholic theological work, 92

on sacramentality, mediation and communion, 112
Merton, Thomas 61, 68f
  on interior solitude, 44
  on spiritual life, 44
  as exemplar of spiritual companion-ship, 115-122
Merton Quarterly, The, 120
Mokshe (freedom), 133
Montaro, Edgardo, 34, 70
Montessori, Maria on the child as con-templative, 57
Moran, Gabriel, 54, 81
  religion distinguished from religious-ness, 22, 48,53
  religion distinguished from faithful-ness, 43
  religious education for spiritual companionship, 55-58
  revelation as speaking and listening in the present, 82f
  and "doctrina," 92
  and revelation as practical (not the-oretical) knowledge, 93
  Church as power structure, 100
  on democratization of the Church, 105
  on mystics, 125
  on the body and moral response, 129
  on teaching, 141
Mystics, 127

Neo-orthodox theological and religious perspective, 32
Newman, John Henry, 9, 32
  on change, 91
Neusner, Jacob, 103
Niebuhr, H. Richard on defensiveness in theological thinking, 76
  on revelation and control, 90
  on revelation and relativity, 90
  on liberal Christianity run amok, 135
Nishmat Hayyim, 128
Nostra Aetate, 37, 120
Novak, David 7
  on absolute truths, 23f 38

supporting exclusive truth claims, 50f
Objectivity in faith, the problem, 88f
Ochs, Carol on divine presence 135f
Orthodox Judaism, Modern, 48
orthodox (small o) theology method and ideology, 32
Orthodoxis, 67, 70
Orthopraxis 67, 70

Panikkar, Raimundo, 3
  on truth claims, 51
Paul VI, Pope, 34, 53
Paul, Saint, gifts of the Holy Spirit, 94
Pawlikowski, John, on anti-Judaism in the Letter to the Hebrews, 20
Pelikan, Jaroslav on tradtions as icons, 52
Pharisees, perushim, separate ones 20
Philo of Alexandria on kindness, 3
P'Kuach Nefesh, 67, 111
Pius IX, Pope, 31, 34
Pius XII, Pope, 31, 34,
Pontifical Biblical Commission, 19
The Pope Against the Jews, by Robert Kertzer
Powers, David on metaphor and naïve realism in theological speech, 65f
Prayer and spiritual companionship, 17, 45
Project for the Contemplative Mind in Society, 127
Probabalism, 111
Prophetic principle, 78
Proportionalism in moral reflection, 66f, 110ff
Principles of Christian Theology, by John Macquarrie

Qu'ran (Koran), 85

Rahner, Karl, 82
  on Trinity, 18
  newness of doctrinal formulation, 41
  on God's radical self-communica-tion, 49

categorical and transcendental revelation, 50

"hearers of the word," 53

and universal availability of revelation, 83

and engagement in revelatory relationship, 85

on changing formulas of doctrine, 91

on loss of spiritual initiative in post-conciliar Church, 100

and Logos christology, 108

faith as trust, 134

Ratzinger, Cardinal Joseph (Benedict XVI, Pope), on Buddhism, 14

Reflections on Covenant and Mission, USCCB, 19

Relativism, fear of, 90f

misconstrued, 51, 63

Religion and Alienation, by Gregory Baum, 77

Religious Freedom, Vatican declaration on, 37

Religious education, dialectical function, 52f

positive on teaching Catholics about Jews (Eric Yoffie), 55

Re-Judaizing Christianity (D. Tracy), 25

and moral views, 109ff

Relaxation Response, The, by Herbert Benson, 127

Religion, distinguished from spirituality, 44ff

neither true nor false religions, 52

Replacement theology (supersessionism), 39

Restorationist papacy of John Paul II, 36f

and Jewish-Christian relations, 37

and triumphalisms, 37f

Return to the Center, by Bede Griffith, OSB, 23

Revelation, 118

Karl Rahner on God's radical self-communciation, 49

and the sacred and the Holy (capital H) distinguished, 49

Macquarrie on epistomology of revelation, 50

Karl Ranher on categorical and transcendental revelation, 50

and the human constitution of religions, 72

moral imperative to reform language of revelation, 77

and Nicholas of Cusa's *doctra ignorant*, 78

and Rosemary Radford Ruether's critical and prophetic principles, 78

Richard P. McBrien on, 78

and violence, 79-82

Cantwell Smith on religion not being revealed, 81

on and mystery in Tillich, 84

and engagement, 85f

in Torah, 85

in Qu'ran, 85

Martin Buber on, 85

and God's self-communciation, 86

Avery Dulles, SJ on, 87

H. Richard Niebuhr on, 80, 90

Augustine of Hippo on mystery of God and, 92

Thomas Aquinas on mystery of God and, 92

Gabriel Moran on, 93

John Hicks on, 93f

as presence in Franz Rosensweig's work, 129

Revelation: The Religions and Violence, by Leo Lefebure, 80

Rilke, Rainer Maria on silence and gratefulness, 131f

Ritschl, Albrecht, 53

"Romantic religion," 139

Robinson, Edward, 49

Rosato, Phlip on eucharist and justice, 114

Rosensweig, Franz, 82

Rothman, Rabbi Murray, 4

Ruah, 18, 128

Sacrificium intellectum, 91

Sacred, distinguished from the Holy (capital H), 49

Salvation, 21
  and sanctification, 104
Schillebeeckx, Edward, 17
Schleiermacher, Fredrick, 53
Schopenhauer Arthur, on compassion, 132
Second Vatican Council, viii, 14
Sedeqah, 114
Segundo, Juan Luis on eucharist, 9
Sensus fidelium,112
Separateness, Jewish 20ff
Seven Storey Mountain, The, by
  Thomas Merton, 119
Shannon, William on Thomas Merton,
  125
Silence and solitude in works of
  Thomas Merton, 121
"Signs of the times," 53
Sloyan, Gerald, Jewish roots of
  Christian morality, 100 –115
  on the novelty of ultramontanism,
  112
  twisting Jesus' moral teaching,
  112f
  Jesus' teaching on justice, 115
Smart, Ninian on religions criticizing
  one another, 46
Smith, William Cantwell on revelation and religion, 81
Samyojana, 130
*Social Theory of Religious Education,
  A*, by George Albert Coe, 53
Solomon, Norman equating liberal
  with relativist, 63f
Soloveitchick, Joseph, 43, 48,112
  on interreligious relations, 32f, 38f
Song of the Self, by Carol Ochs, 139.
Spirituality, distinguised from religion, 44ff
Splendor Veritas (The Splendor of
  Truth), by Pope John Paul II, 66
Star of Redemption, The by Franz
  Rosensweig, 82
Stein, Edith, 34
Steinberg, David on Judaism's rejection of dualism, 103
  on Judaism's moral realism, 111ff
Stendahl, Krister, 59f

"Holy envy," 8
  and the next step in Jewish-
  Christian relations, 43
  and James Carroll's book
  Constantine's Sword, 77
Sunyata, 128, 133
Supersession (replacement theology),
  39
Sufis on silence, 131
  on knowing, 134
Suzuki, Shunryu, 2
Swidler, Leonard, 71, 76
  and the age of dialogue , 79
  fear of relativism, 90f
Symbol, Jesus as symbol of God, 106f.
Synod of Bishops (1971), 113

"Teaching of contempt," 38
Thich Nhat Hanh, 6, 133
  on mindfulness, 129f
Thurman, Robert on contemplation
  and social justice, 137
Tillich, Paul, 135
  religions pointing beyond themselves, 41
  and mystery, 84
  criticized by Heschel, 135
Toaff, Elio, 33
Torah, 85
Tracy, David, 53, 67
  on re-Judaizing of Christianity, 4
  on the praxis of interreligious dialogue, 9
  on the liberal model for theological
  reflection, 13
Traditions as icons, (J. Pelikan), 52
Truth claims, human constitution of,
  51
  as property, 58
  liberation and renouncing absolute
  truth claims, 51f
  and the mystery of God, 84f
  Heschel on, 85
Triumphalism, 37f, 40, 49
  of memory and of pain among Jews,
  54
  John XXIII's rejection of, 102
  and ultramontanism, 112

"Unitive pluralism," (Paul Knitter), 47
Upeksha, 133

Veverke, Fayette Breaux on bridges
    and boundaries in interreligious
    relations, 57f
von Beeck, Franz Joseph on searching
    for objectivity in faith, 88f
von Rad, Gerhard on justice in the
    "Old testament," 114

Welty, Eudora, 82
*We Remember: Reflections on the
    Shoah*, The Vatican, 62
Whitehead, Alfred North, on noticing
    the obvious, 77
Whitson, Robley, on the coming con-
    vergence of world religions, 40
Wills, Garry on *We Remember*, 34
    on Augustine of Hippo, 65
    on Augustine as model bishop , 101f
    on official Church claims that
    "make a sophomore blush," 90
Weston Priory, 114
Wolfson, Elliot on Jewish and Christian
    incarnationalism, 105ff
Women's ordination, 89
Worship and justice in Judaism and
    Christianity, 113f
    Segundo on, 114
    Merton on contemplative founda-
    tions for, 143

Yoffie, Eric, on positive Jewish educa-
    tion about Catholics and
    Catholicism, 55

Zazen, 5
Zohar, 20